An Alphabet of Books

Literature-Based Activities for Schools and Libraries

By Robin Works Davis

Alleyside Press

Fort Atkinson, Wisconsin

Acknowledgements

Unless otherwise noted, the songs, fingerplays, and poems presented here are original or come from the storytelling tradition. Every effort has been made to find the original sources of the materials. If errors have been made, they will be corrected in future editions.

I wish to thank the many talented authors and illustrators of the quality children's literature included in this work.

Thank you to the staff of the Hurst Public Library for their support while writing this reference.

Warms thanks and love to my husband, Les.

Published by Alleyside Press, an imprint of Highsmith Press
Highsmith Press
W5527 Highway 106
P.O. Box 800
Fort Atkinson, Wisconsin 53538-0800
1-800-558-2110

© Robin Works Davis, 1995
Cover design: Frank Neu

The paper used in this publication meets the minimum requirements of American National Standard for Information Science — Permanence of Paper for Printed Library Material. ANSI/NISO Z39.48-1992.

Library of Congress Cataloging in Publication

Davis, Robin Works, 1962–
    An alphabet of books: literature-based activities for schools and libraries / by Robin Works Davis.
      p. cm.
    Includes bibliographical references.
    ISBN 0-917846-38-9 (alk. paper)
    1. Language arts (Elementary)--United States. 2. Activity programs in education--United States. 3. Reading (Elementary)--United States--Language experience approach. 4. Children--United States--Books and reading. I. Title.
    LB1576.D238 1995
    372.6'0973--dc20   94-37600

Contents

Introduction

An Alphabet of Books: Literature-Based Activities for Schools and Libraries is designed to help librarians, teachers, storytellers and other adults create meaningful and exciting story hours and programs. The stories and activities focus on themes about animals or other natural elements and will be of greatest interest to children in preschool through grade two.

Each theme has been developed with three important goals in mind: The first is the need for simple, inexpensive or free activities for teachers or librarians to use as extensions to a child's experience with literature. The meaning of extension is to stretch the story, to magnify the child's understanding and enjoyment of a book. Literature can be extended through music, media, drama, art and language. Art experiences especially help children to internalize a tale.

The second goal is to provide the stimulation children's imaginations need in order to develop their creative ability. Stimulation can be provided through activities such as stories, creative dramatics, music, puppets, crafts and other projects. Creativity and language development can both be enhanced when experiences with literature are presented as a part of the total communication process. This means including speaking, listening, writing, music and math as part of the experience.

The third goal is to suggest materials to help the teacher, librarian, or storyteller create the reading friendly environment that is known as "Whole Language." Whole language is a perspective on language and language acquisition. It espouses the idea that children learn language through frequent and varied opportunities to use that language. It involves children in using all modes of communication, including reading, writing, listening, experiencing, illustrating and doing to learn language. Whole language also emphasizes that the opportunities must be real, natural and paired with other activities such as social studies, music, the arts and dramatic play that are responses to the literature experience. The activities herein seek to make a young child's literature experience meaningful by including developmentally appropriate, related, creative ideas. The activities are also designed to accommodate a variety of environments, including the classroom, library, or day care. The activities can be used for self discovery, or be adult directed. Furthermore, the activities are not limited to the books and other items listed—they can easily be adapted to other materials.

The literature-based activities will:

Provide inexpensive or free patterns or activities for librarians and teachers to extend literature experiences in the storytime or classroom setting.

Develop children's interpretive skills.

Develop powers of creative expression through artistic play.

Enhance story memory and enjoyment.

Enhance children's language development through literature extension activities.

Promote awareness of the function of language.

Provide teachers with ideas for incorporating literature into the curriculum of art, music and language arts.

Outline

The book is arranged alphabetically with a theme from a selected children's book accompanying each letter. The themes are all animals or other objects found in nature. These concrete themes will help the user by allowing them to illustrate the theme with the actual object or pictures. Each letter of the alphabet has the following elements:

Theme: For organization and to link the activities presented together for unity and flow. To present a cohesive, in-depth look at the subject of the particular literature selection.

Literature Selection: The book that will be the focus of literature sharing and theme. An annotation is included. All titles cited in this book have been well reviewed and selected from current or classic children's literature commonly available in school and public libraries. Sources used to choose titles include *School Library Journal, A to Zoo: Subject Access to Children's Picture Books, Booklist* and *Kirkus Reviews*. The literature chosen is only a small portion of the quality literature that is available.

Warm-Up Activities: To focus children on the theme and literature, to settle the children in for a story, to encourage participation and to set the mood. Warm ups include activities such as rhymes, fingerplays, chants, songs and music. Children especially enjoy singing and rhythmic activities.

Poetry: To expand the theme, to introduce children to different kinds of language patterns and words, to develop a feeling for rhythm, rhyme, meter, etc.

Language Experience: To connect the oral and written word, to allow the child to see their own words in print, to incorporate the learning of reading and writing. Language experience includes activities such as letter dictating, recording children's ideas or reactions, labeling, group stories or poetry and lists.

Creative Dramatics: To develop body awareness and important motor skills through play. To develop self expression and character identification. To enhance self esteem.

Literature-Based Activity Pattern or Idea: To immerse the child in the literary experience, to expand understanding of the story, to expand creativity, to improve story memory, to develop fine motor skills. The approximate cost per child is included. These prices are based on current materials costs at the time of publication. Prices also assume that basic tools, such as scissors, pencils and glue, are already owned.

Nametag Pattern: To promote name recognition, identity and a sense of being special to the children participating in the storytime or literature activity.

Additional Literature Selections: To fill out the storytime or program, more books on the theme have been listed.

A note about special needs children

This reference assumes that those who work with differently abled children will have access to specialized materials for use in one on one activities. These materials include special scissors, hand braces, book holders, crayon holders, large print or braille books, etc. All of the activities can be adapted for use with special equipment.

 A is for Armadillo

The Armadillo is a strange but interesting creature! This scaly, nine-banded creature is also called a "Texas Turkey" and a "Hoover Hog."

The Armadillo from Amarillo

By Lynn Cherry. (Harcourt Brace Jovanovich, 1994)

Charming watercolor and oil pictures of Texas scenes and rhymed verse tell the story of a curious armadillo. Sasparillo Armadillo explores the state of Texas from San Antonio to Amarillo. Great story for introducing the state's culture, geography and scientific information.

❏ Warm-Up Activities

Fingerplay

Five Armadillos
Five armadillos walking into town
(hold up five fingers and walk)
Along came a tornado and blew one around!
(turn around)
"Oh!" said the rest,
(put hands on face and say "Oh!")
"We must do our best
To not be blown to the ground."
(jump down to the ground)
Repeat with 4, 3, 2, 1.

Chant

Armadillo, Armadillo
Armadillo, armadillo, my oh my,
See the little termite sneaking by?
Armadillo, armadillo, crunch, crunch, crunch!
Yum! I guess you swallowed your lunch.
Repeat with ant, caterpillar, worm, beetle.

Song

What Can You Do, Armadillo?
(Sung to the tune of "What Can You Do, Ponchinella?")
What can you do, armadillo, armadillo?
What can you do, armadillo funny you?
Oh, I can eat an ant, armadillo, armadillo.
I can eat an ant, armadillo, funny you!

(Repeat with various things an armadillo might do, such as scratch the ground, run from a car, jump up high, etc.)

❏ Follow-Up Activities

Poetry

Armadillos
One or two armadillos underground,
Three or four armadillo pups are found.
Five or six armadillos jump in the air,
Seven, eight, when armadillos get a scare.
Nine, ten, armadillos are my friend,
Okay, now let's count them all again.

Language Experience

Armadillos have very unusual bodies. Use the book *The Complete, Unabridged Armadillo Handbook* to label the parts. Introduce new vocabulary, such as snout, scales, bands, balloon stomach, etc.

Creative Dramatics

The story *The Adventures of L.A.* by M.M. Dee makes a charming mini play about armadillos.

Literature-Based Activity: Baggy Armadillo

Supplies: Pattern, glue, scissors, yarn, and crayons.
Directions: Copy pattern for each child. Color and cut out. Give each child a lunch sack that is still folded flat. Glue the top snout to the bottom of the folded bag. Glue the bottom snout on the side of the bag directly under the top snout. Draw claw-like feet and scales on the front and back of the sack. Add a yarn tail.
Cost per armadillo: 5¢

❏ Additional Literature Selections

Abernathy, Francis. *How the Critters Created Texas.* Hendrick Long Publishers, 1982.

Boynton, Sandra. *But Not the Hippopotamus*. Simon and Schuster, 1982.

Cased, Mary Brooke. *Blue Bonnet at the Alamo*. Hendrick Long Publishers, 1993.

Dee, M. M. *The Adventures of L.A.* Hendrick Long Publishers, 1983

Fannin, Angela. *The Complete Unabridged Armadillo Handbook*. Eakin Press, 1982.

Lavies, Bianca. *It's an Armadillo*. Dutton, 1989.

Luttrell, Ida. *Not Like That, Armadillo*. Harcourt Brace Jovanovich, 1982.

Monsell, Mary Elise. *Armadillo*. Atheneum, 1991.

Singer, Marilyn. *Archer Armadillo's Secret Room*. Macmillan, 1985.

Stuart, Dee. *The Astonishing Armadillo*. Carolrhoda, 1993.

Warren, Cathy. *The Ten Alarm Campout*. Lothrop, Lee, and Shepherd, 1983.

Armadillo Nametag

Baggy Armadillo

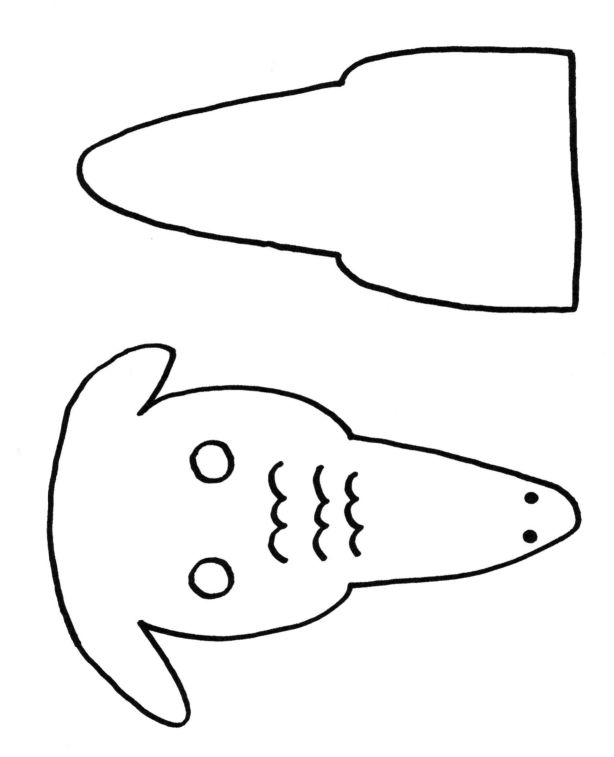

B is for Bat

Bats are very important to the ecosystem! One mouse eared bat can eat thousands of mosquitoes in a single night. Bats also pollinate plants by carrying pollen as they fly.

Stellaluna

By Janell Cannon. (Harcourt Brace, 1993)

Stellaluna is baby bat who is separated from her mother when an owl chases them. Stellaluna flies until she is very tired, then she falls into a birds nest. There, she and the birds teach each other their ways until she is finally reunited with her mother. Adorable bird and bat faces grace the watercolor illustrations.

❏ Warm-Up Activities

Fingerplay

A big black bat
(lock thumbs together and flap fingers as wings)
Comes flying through the night.
(swoop arms up and down)
As he zoomed past me, it was quite a scary sight.
But I don't care
(shrug shoulders)
If he's flying in the air,
(point up)
I'm safe and sound, hiding under a chair!
(squat down and put hands over head)

Song

Use "The Bat Has a Beep," from *The Zoo Comes to School: Fingerplays and Action Rhymes*, Josephine Colville, Macmillan, 1973, p. 10.

❏ Follow-Up Activities

Poetry

Bats
Imagine that!
A squeaky bat.
They fly, they swoop, they see at night,
They do not like it when it's bright.
They can hear the tiny bug sounds,
And when they sleep, they are upside down.

Language Experience

Make a chart of contrasts and comparisons of bats and birds. Begin by making two columns on a large sheet of paper or poster board, one labeled "birds," and one labeled "Bats." Have the children list what they know about each creature, for example birds have feathers, bats have fur, both fly, both eat bugs, etc.

Creative Dramatics

Have the children stand on their heads one at a time with an adult spotting them. Ask them what it would be like to sleep upside down. Also try turning off the lights and ask questions about being able to locate objects using a bat's "radar."

Caves are an interesting topic that go along with bats. Cover a table or climbing structure with a blanket or parachute to make a cave. Or, make an obstacle course of different kinds of terrain that might be found in a cave, such as a narrow passage, or a large damp cavern.

Literature-Based Activities: Upside Down Bat Cup

Supplies: Pattern, one paper cup, glue, scissors, a white crayon or chalk, and one sheet of black construction paper.
Directions: Using the pattern and the white crayon, trace or draw the bat wings and eyes on the black paper and cut out. Glue the wings and eyes to the inverted cup. The bats can be hung by poking a hole in the bottom and stringing yarn through.
Cost per bat: 6¢

Ears and Hearing

Supplies: Construction paper, scissors, glue or tape.
Directions: Discuss bats special hearing called *echolocation*. Cut bat and other animal ears and headbands from construction paper to fit the children. Use the book *Heads* and pay attention to the ears and the direction they point on the animals. Cut rabbit, elephant, donkey, bat, pig, and others.

Compare and contrast the different kinds of ears. Let them choose the kind of ears they would like. Let the children trace or design their own.
Cost: 1¢

Adopt a Bat!

For more information write to:
Bat Conservation International
PO Box 162603
Austin, TX 78716

❏ Additional Literature Selections

Althea. *Bats: Based on the Long Eared Bat.* Longman Group, 1988.

Bash, Barbara. *Shadows of Night.* Sierra Club, 1993.

Chichester, Clark. *Lunch With Aunt Augusta.* Dial, 1992.

Goor, Ron and Nancy. *Heads.* Atheneum, 1988.

Hoban, Russell. *Lavinia Bat.* Holt, 1984.

Horowitz, Ruth. *Bat Time.* Four Winds, 1991.

Kerbo, Ronal. *Caves.* Children's Press, 1981.

Mollel, Tololwa. *A Promise to the Sun: A Story of Africa.* Little Brown, 1992.

Pringle, Laurence. *Vampire Bats.* Morrow, 1992.

Selsam, Millicent. *A First Look at Bats.* Walker, 1991.

Ungerer, Tomi. *Rufus.* Dell, 1961.

Bat Nametag

Upside Down Bat Cup

Wing—Cut 2

C *is for* **Crow**

Make a pine cone "Crow Feeder" and hang it outside a window! Cover a large pine cone with sugarless peanut butter. Roll the pine cone in a pan filled with inexpensive bird seed. Tie with yarn by the tip.

Black Crow, Black Crow

By Ginger F. Guy. (Greenwillow, 1991)

A black crow caws outside the window of a small girl throughout the day. The girl wonders what the crow's call means, and imagines a mother crow and her fledglings. Childlike simple watercolors of the personified, happy crows are featured throughout.

❏ Warm-Up Activities

Fingerplay

Five Little Crows
Five little crows in an old oak tree,
A father *(hold up thumb)*
A mother *(hold up pointer)*
And babies three. *(hold up remaining three fingers)*
Father brought a worm, *(point to thumb)*
Mother brought a bug, *(point to pointer)*
And the three crow babies started to tug;
This one ate the bug, "*Gulp!*" *(point to middle finger)*
This one ate the worm, "*Gulp!*" *(point to ring finger)*
And this baby crow just waits his turn. *(point to little finger)*

Song/Music

"Two Little Crows"

(To the tune of "Two Little Blackbirds")
Two little crows sitting on a hill,
One named Mack and the other named Bill.
Fly away Mack, fly away Bill;
Come back Mack, come back Bill.
Two little crows sitting on a hill,
One named Mack and the other named Bill.

❏ Follow-Up Activities

Poetry

Crow
Caw! Caw! Caw!
Says the big black crow.
He likes to be
Where the farmer's corn grows.
Caw! Caw! Caw!
What a noisy bird.
With the *ugliest* song
I've ever heard!

Language Experience

The crows in the story *Black Crow, Black Crow* are dressed and acting like people in the story. Ask the children what they know about how real crows act. What do they eat? Do they really sleep in beds? Do crows wear clothes? What kind of covering do they have on their body? Enlarge the nametag pattern to poster size and record the children's answers as they give them. A book to use as a general reference about birds and to expand this theme is *Birdwise: Forty Fun Feats for Finding Out About Our Feathered Friends* by Pamela Hickman, Addison-Wesley, 1988.

Display a feather collection with a magnifying glass. Let the children describe the colors and patterns they see. Point out the quill and barbs on the feather. Use *My Feather* or *The Feather Book* for more ideas.

Creative Dramatics

Now that you have discussed what real crows are like, have the children do some dramatics. Use comparisons of how people do things and how birds do things. For example, have them pretend to make dinner, set the table and eat. Then they can pretend to be a crow catching its dinner, flying home, and feeding its fledglings.

Literature-Based Activity: Fanciful Flying Crow

Supplies: Two pieces of 9" x 12" black construction paper, chalk, scissors, glue.

Directions: Cut a 3" x 12" strip of black paper for the body and a 3" x 6" strip for the head. Trace or copy crow pattern onto scrap poster board and cut them out. This is a pattern that can be traced on each child's other sheet of black construction paper. Cut out the wings, tail, feet, and beak. Each child will glue the two strips previously cut into circles. Put a small amount of glue on one end of each strip and hold together for a few seconds until it is dry. Now glue the two circles together so they form a figure eight with the smaller circle on top. This is the crow's body. Now glue the beak, wings, tail, and feet to the body. Put glue on the "X" and attach as shown in the picture. Draw eyes on with the chalk. A wire can be hung across your story space so the crows can sit on it. Attach them with tape.

Cost per crow: 8¢

Bird Watch

Gather up various pictures of eggs, actual nests, some binoculars, and bird seed. Go on a bird watching trip or simply put food on a window sill and watch through the window. Record the kinds of birds that are seen by drawing or writing their names.

❏ Additional Literature Selections

Dillon, Jana. *Jeb Scarecrow's Pumpkin Patch.* Houghton Mifflin, 1992.

Greenstein, Elaine. *Emily and the Crows.* Picture Book Studio, 1992.

Hale, Irina. *The Naughty Crow.* Macmillan, 1992.

Holder, Heidi. *Crows: An Old Rhyme.* Farrar, Strauss, & Giroux, 1987.

Lionni, Leo. *Six Crows.* Random House, 1988.

Mainwaring, Jane. *My Feather.* Doubleday, 1989.

Marion, Jeff. *Hello Crow.* Orchard Watts, 1990.

O'Connor, Karen. *The Feather Book.* Dillon, 1990.

Skofield, James. *Crow Moon, Worm Moon.* Four Winds Press, 1990.

VanLaan, Nancy. *Rainbow Crow.* Knopf, 1989.

Wolff, Ashely. *A Year of Birds.* Dodd Mead, 1984.

Yashima, Taro. *Crow Boy.* Viking, 1955.

Crow Nametag

Fanciful Flying Crow

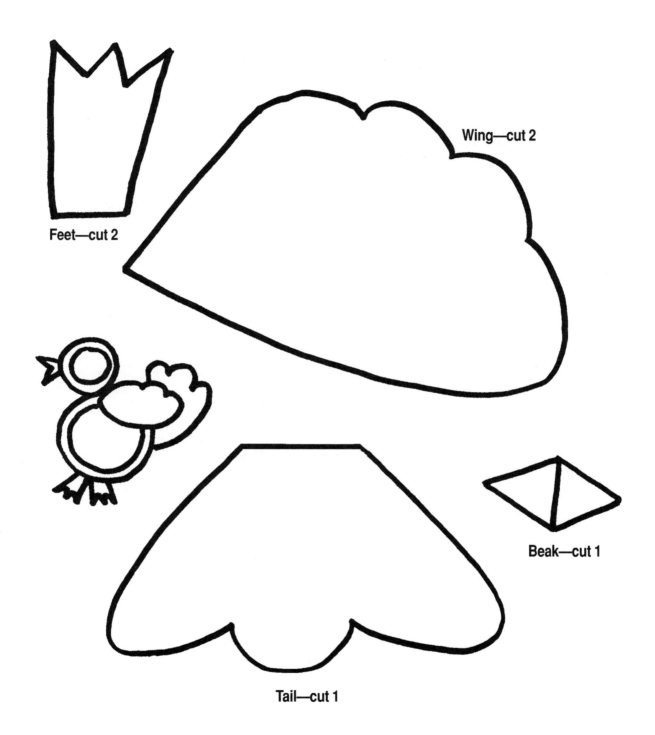

Feet—cut 2

Wing—cut 2

Beak—cut 1

Tail—cut 1

 *is for* **Donkey**

Donkeys are members of the horse family. A female donkey is called a "Jenny" and a male is a "Jack."

The Donkey's Tale

By Joanne Oppenheim. (Bantam, 1991)

A rhyming retelling of the classic fable on following too much advice. An old farmer and his son travel to town to sell their donkey. In the end, they learn their lesson about the opinions of others. Delightful water-color illustrations are by Chris Demarest.

❏ Warm-Up Activities

Fingerplay

Shoe the Donkey

Shoe the donkey,
Shoe the donkey,
(point to feet)
See if she will ride.
Will she carry a sack
Upon her back?
(sling an imaginary bag over your shoulder)
If she will,
Give her grain,
(pretend to eat)
If she won't
Go home again.
(wave goodbye)

Rhyme

I have a little donkey,
His name is dapple grey.
I lent him to my best friend
To ride a mile away.
She rode him in a mud puddle,
She rode him through the town.
And now my little donkey,
His name is Dapple Brown!

Song

The Donkey Says

(To the tune of "The Wheels on the Bus")
The donkey says hee haw,

Hee, haw, haw,
Hee, haw, haw,
The donkey says hee haw haw,
all through the town.
Repeat with:
The donkey's hooves go clop, clop, clop.
The donkey's tail goes swish, swish, swish, etc.

❏ Follow-Up Activities

Poetry

See the Donkey

See the donkey
A grey donkey.
I ride him every day.
See the donkey
Braying donkey.
As he looks my way.
When I give the donkey
An apple to eat
Trot, trot, trot
Go his hoofed little feet.

Language Experience

Create a story with a pattern similar to that of *The Donkey's Tale*. Perhaps it could be about an animal who takes too much advice from humans and gets into trouble. An example is a rabbit who paints himself different colors on the advice of helpful children, but gets caught by a fox.

Creative Dramatics

Use the reader's theater script featuring a donkey, "The Bremen Town Musicians," from *Reader's Theater for Beginning Readers,* p. 37-40, by Suzanne I. Barchers, Teacher Ideas Press, 1993.

Literature-Based Activity: Standing Donkey

Supplies: Pattern, two spring-type clothespins, brown posterboard, brown markers.

Directions: Cut out one copy of donkey body from the brown posterboard for each child. Have the children use brown markers to color the clothespins brown. Clip the clothespins on the donkey body to complete the animals.

❏ Additional Literature Selections

"The Biyera Well," p. 90-93, from *Look Back and See* by Margaret Read MacDonald, HW Wilson, 1991.

Brenner, Barbara. *The Donkey's Dream*. Philomel, 1985.

Cohen, Barbara. *The Donkey's Story*. Lothrop, 1988.

Hale, Irina. *Donkey's Dreadful Day*. Atheneum, 1982.

Hays, Barbara. *Donkey Skin*. Rourke, 1984.

McClure, Gillian. *The Christmas Donkey*. Farrar, Strauss, and Giroux, 1993.

Maris, Ron. *Hold Tight, Bear!* Delacourte, 1989.

Morpurgo, Micheal. *Jo-Jo the Melon Donkey*. Prentice Hall, 1988.

Pilling, Ann. *Donkey's Day Out*. Lion Press, 1990.

"Please All...Please None," p. 68-72, from *Look Back and See* by Margaret Read MacDonald, HW Wilson, 1991.

Potter, Tessa. *Donkeys*. Macmillan, 1989.

Donkey Nametag

Standing Donkey

E is for *Elephant*

Elephants can make and hear sounds that are too low for human hearing. This is one way in which they communicate with each other. Elephants can call their friends over 2 ½ miles— Can you?

Bill's Belly Button

By Anita Jeram. (Little Brown, 1991)

Everyone loves Bill, the friendly elephant that lives in the park. But one day Bill notices that he can't find his belly button! Charming, light watercolor illustrations of the elephant and children complete this sweet tale.

❏ Warm-Up Activities

Fingerplay

Five Big Elephants

Five big elephants marching through a glade,
(hold up five fingers)
The first one said, "Let's stop in the shade."
(point to thumb)
The second one said, "The day is getting hotter."
(point to pointer finger)
The third one said, "Let's get a cool drink of water."
(point to middle finger)
The fourth one said, "The water is far away."
(point to ring finger)
The fifth one said, "I'll show you the way."
(point to little finger)
Then all five elephants walked in a line,
(move five fingers as if walking)
They got a drink of water and they're doing just fine!

Action Rhyme

The Elephant

The elephant goes like this and that;
(swing both arms in front while bending over)
He's terribly big,
(raise arms above head)
And terribly fat.
(hold arms out to sides)
He has no fingers,
(wiggle fingers)
He has no toes
(point to toes)
But goodness gracious what a nose!
(hold one arm in front like a trunk)

Song

Use *One Elephant, Deux Elephants* by Sharon, Lois, and Bram, Elephant Record, 1978

❏ Follow-Up Activities

Poetry

Old One

Old wise elephant
Stands on the plain
Her ears move slowly
Back and forth like
Wings of a giant butterfly.
Old wise elephant
Stands and thinks so deeply.
Oh, wise one
What do you know?

Language Experience

Create a long poem. Cut out long strips of grey paper and have the children dictate or write poems on them. Tape them together end to end to create a long "trunk."

After sharing the story about Bill the elephant, share some elephant facts. Ask the kids if they think elephants really do have belly buttons. Two good resources on elephants are *The World of Elephants* by Virginia Harrison, Gareth Stevens, 1989; and *Endangered Species: Elephants* by Peter Jackson, Chartwell Books, 1990.

Creative Dramatics

For dramatics, you will need a long rope and *Animal Alphabet Songs* by David S. Polansky, Perfect Score

Music, 1982 (cassette). Any other appropriate music, such as "Baby Elephant Walk" will also do. Have the children line up and hold on to the rope. Tell them they are elephants and the rope is their tails and trunks. Have them "elephant walk" around to the music.

Literature-Based Activity: Elephant Paper Plate Puppets

Supplies: Pattern, two 1" x 14" strips of gray paper, one 2 ½" circle of gray paper, one 11" x 17" piece of gray paper, one paper plate, scissors, glue, and a black crayon.

Directions: Glue the two strips of paper together at right angles. (See pattern for assistance.) Fold strip "A" over strip "B" until you run out of paper. Glue the other end together to hold it in place. This is the trunk. Draw nostrils on the gray circle and glue it to one end of the trunk. Glue the other end to the paper plate and let dry. Cut out two ear shapes from the large piece of gray paper and glue to the back of the plate so they show in front. Draw eyes and a mouth, and your elephant puppet is finished.

Cost per puppet: 12¢

❏ Additional Literature Selections

Arnold, Caroline. *Elephant.* Morrow, 1993.

Barnes, Jill. *Elephant Rescue.* Garrett, 1990.

McKee, David. Elmer: *The Story of a Patchwork Elephant.* Lothrop, 1989.

Propp, Jim. *Tuscanini.* Bradbury, 1992.

Richardson, Judith. *The Way Home.* Macmillan, 1991.

Riddell, Chris. *The Trouble With Elephants.* Harper Trophy, 1988.

Sheppard, Jeff. *The Right Number of Elephants.* Harper Trophy, 1990.

Smath, Jerry. *But No Elephants.* Parents Magazine Press, 1979.

Vipont, Elfrida. *The Elephant and the Bad Baby.* Putnam, 1986.

Elephant Nametag

Elephant Puppet

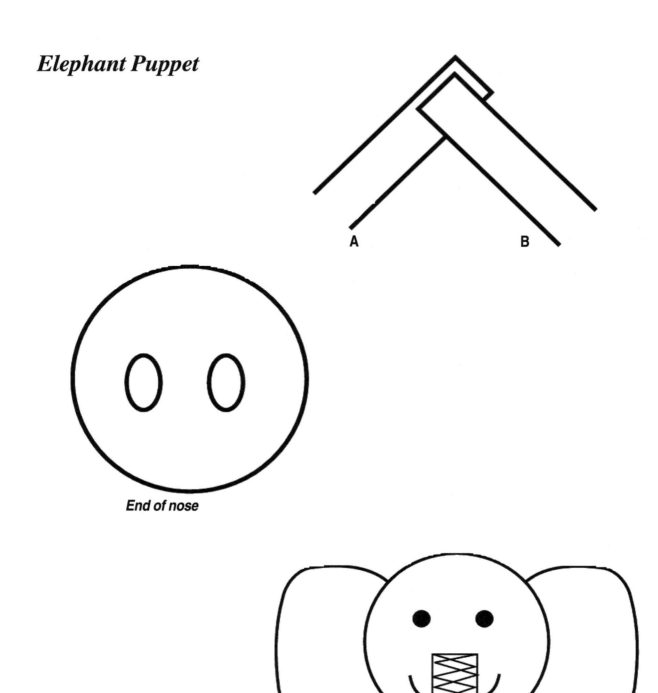

End of nose

A

B

 **F** *is for* **Fox**

A fox is a bushy tailed member of the dog family. There are red, gray, brown and white foxes. Foxes live in dens and can be found in the Arctic, Asia, Europe, North and South America.

Grandfather Tang's Story

Anne Tompert. (Crown, 1990)

Grandfather Tang tells a story about shape-changing fox fairies using the storytelling device of tangrams. The foxes, Chou and Wu Ling, try to outdo each other by changing into many different animal forms. Finally, a hunter stops their foolish game.

❑ Warm-Up Activities

Fingerplays

Put your finger in the fox's hole,
(make a circle with one hand and put index finger of other hand into it)
But fox is not at home.
(shrug shoulders)
Fox is by the back door
Picking at a bone!
(turn around and "pick" at the air)

Two Foxes

Two little foxes
Lying in a heap
(hold up two fingers)
Soft and furry,
Fast asleep.
(rest head on hands)
Along comes a hound
Sniffing at the ground,
("walk" fingers of one hand up the other arm)
The hound starts to bay, "*Howwwwwwwrrrrrr!*"
The foxes run away!
(put hands behind back)

Song

Use "Fox Went Out on a Chilly Night," from *Wee Silly Songs* by Pamella Beall and Susan Nipp, Price Stern Sloan, 1992.

Or, "Fox" from *Animal Alphabet Songs* by David Polansky, Perfect Score Music, 1982. (PO Box 5061, Cochituate, MA 01778.)

❑ Follow-Up Activities

Poetry

Fox

Tall ears
Black nose
Fluffy tail
Quick he goes.
Brownish orange
Tail tufted white
Chase a rabbit
Late at night.

Language Experience

Have the children make a list of all the different things a fox might eat in the wild, such as rabbits, mice, bugs, fruit, etc.

Creative Dramatics

Compare different stories that have foxes, such as *What's in Fox's Sack?* and *One Fine Day*. Are the foxes tricky in different stories? Pick a simple fox story, such as *What's in Foxes Sack?* to act out.

Literature-Based Activity: Seated Fox

Supplies: Pattern, 8" x 8" square of newspaper or other lightweight paper.
Directions: Follow the folding directions on pattern.
Cost per fox: 1¢

❑ Additional Literature Selections

Arnosky, Jim. *Watching Foxes.* Lothrop, 1984.

Bergman, Donna. *City Fox.* Macmillan, 1992.

Fox, Mem. *Hattie and the Fox*. Macmillan, 1992.

Galdone, Paul. *What's in Fox's Sack*? Houghton
    Mifflin, 1984.

Giffard, Hannah. *Red Fox*. Dial, 1991.

Ling, Mary. *Fox*. Dorling Kindersley, 1992.

McKissack, Patricia. *Flossie and the Fox*. Dial, 1986,

Mason, Cherie. *Wild Fox*. Downeast Books, 1993.

Spier, Peter. *Fox Went Out on a Chilly Night*.
    Doubleday, 1989.

Tejima, Keizaboro. *Fox's Dream*. Putnam, 1987.

Watson, Clyde. *Fox and the Apple Pie*. Harper
    Collins, 1972.

Fox Nametag

Seated Fox

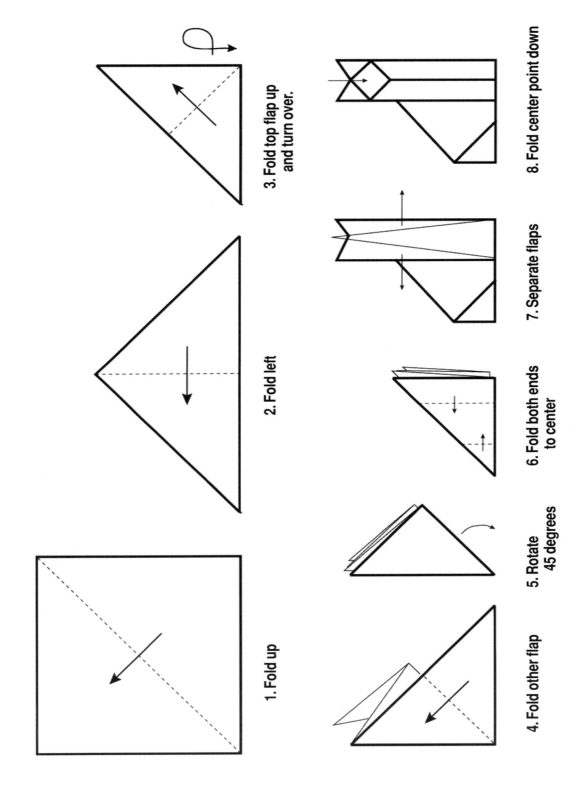

3. Fold top flap up
and turn over.

2. Fold left

1. Fold up

8. Fold center point down

7. Separate flaps

6. Fold both ends
to center

5. Rotate
45 degrees

4. Fold other flap

G is for Goose

I met a goose along my way,
He greeted me with a "Honk!"
I was so surprised that day—
I didn't know geese could talk!

The Missing Mother Goose

By Stephen Krensky. (Doubleday, 1991)

Seven Mother Goose rhymes are expanded into humorous stories. Rhymes include "Little Miss Muffet," "Humpty Dumpty," and "Hey Diddle." Chris Demarest provides colorful and energetic illustrations.

❏ Warm-Up Activities

Fingerplay

Five Little Goslings

Five little goslings, by the barn door,
One swam away and then there were four.
Four little goslings, sitting by a tree,
One swam away and then there were three.
Three little goslings, looking at you,
One swam away, and then there were two.
Two little goslings, lying in the sun,
One swam away and then there was one.
One little gosling, sitting all alone,
He swam away and then there were none.
(Hold up five, four, three, two, and one finger)

Song

"The Grey Goose" from *Burl Ives Sings The Little White Duck and Other Children's Favorites*, Columbia Records, 1974.

❏ Follow-Up Activities

Poetry

"Something Told the Wild Geese" by Rachel Field (Can be found in *The Random House Book of Poetry for Children* by Jack Prelutsky, Random House, 1983, p. 85)

Something told the wild geese
It was time to go.
Though the fields lay golden
Something whispered— "Snow."
Leaves were green and stirring,
Berries, luster glossed,
But beneath warm feathers
Something cautioned— "Frost."
All the sagging orchards
Steamed with amber spice,
But each wild breast stiffened
At remembered ice.
Something told the wild geese
It was time to fly—
Summer sun was on their wings,
Winter in their cry.

Language experience

After sharing several of the stories, it is the perfect opportunity to compose a group expanded nursery rhyme. Get the children started by asking them questions about the rhyme you will use. For example, Why did Little Bo Peep lose her sheep? What did she look like? How did she come to be a shepherdess? Some other rhymes to use are "Little Jack Horner," "Old Mother Hubbard," and "Jack and Jill."

Creative dramatics

Mother Goose and other nursery rhymes make wonderful playlets for children. "Hey Diddle" can be done with a picture of a cat, a fiddle, a cow, the moon, and a dog. Use a real dish and spoon. "The House That Jack Built" can be done with props such as hats, paper cow horns, paper rat ears, and a sack over the head of the child who is the sack of malt.

Literature-Based Activity: Unflappable Paper Goose

Supplies: Pattern, two paper fasteners or brads, tape, one sheet of white paper, an orange and a black crayon, and one orange pipe cleaner.

Directions: Copy or trace pattern onto the white paper and cut out. Be sure and cut two wings! Color the beak orange and draw an eye on the goose shape. Color both sides of the goose. Bend the pipe cleaner to form feet and attach to the goose with tape. Use the brad to attach the wing to the body at the "X." *Cost per goose: 5¢*

❏ Additional Literature Selections

Foreman, Micheal. *Micheal Foreman's Mother Goose*. Harcourt, Brace, Jovanovich, 1991.

Ikeda, Daisaku. *The Snow Country Prince*. Knopf, 1990.

Larrick, Nancy. *Songs from Mother Goose*. Harper and Row, 1989.

Lindberg, Reeve. *The Day the Goose Got Loose*. Dial, 1990.

The Little Dog Laughed and Other Nursery Rhymes. Dutton, 1989.

Marshall, James. *James Marshall's Mother Goose*. Farrar, Strauss, and Giroux, 1979.

Polacco, Patricia. *Rechenka's Eggs*. Putnam, 1988.

Selsam, Millicent. *A First Look at Ducks, Geese, and Swans*. Walker and Company, 1990.

Taylor, E.J. *Goose Eggs*. Candlewick, 1992.

Goose Nametag

Unflappable Paper Goose

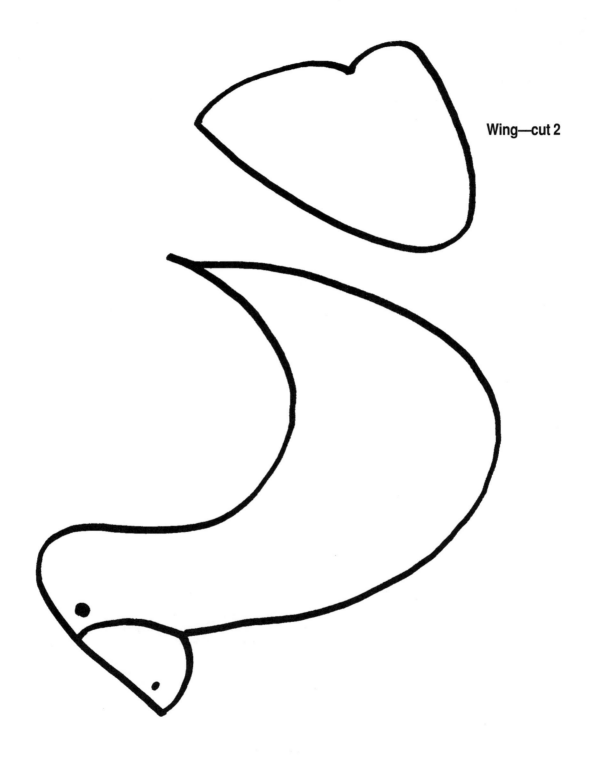

Wing—cut 2

 **is for Hippo**

A hippo should go on a diet—
It's not healthy to be too fat.
But would you want to be the one
To tell a hippo that?

Hot Hippo

By Mwenye Hadithi. (Little Brown, 1986)

Hippo is always hot! So he asks Ngai, the god of everything, to let him live in the river. Ngai is worried about the grass and little fishes. But hippo promises not to eat them. A folkloric explanation of why hippos live in the river and only open their mouths wide above water.

❏ Warm-Up Activities

Fingerplays

A hippo eats grass *(eat)*
A hippo eats hay *(eat)*
A hippo swims and suns all day *(move arms as if swimming)*
A hippo has a round body, head and nose, *(point to body, head and nose)*
He even has ten round toes *(point to toes)*

"One Little Hippo Brought a Blanket" from *Tickle Toe Rhymes* by Joan Knight, Orchard, 1989, p. 36.

Song

"Hippo is Heavy" from *Animal Antics* by Hap Palmer, Activity Records, 1986.

"Hippo" from *Animal Alphabet Songs*, David Polansky, Perfect Score Music, 1982.

Did You Ever See a Hippo

(To the tune of "Did You Ever See a Lassie")
Did you ever see a hippo, a hippo, a hippo,
Did you ever see a hippo, for they are so fat.
For they are fat, they are large and they're huge.
Did you ever see a hippo, for they are so fat.

❏ Follow-Up Activities

Poetry

Hippo Hippo

Hippo, hippo in the lake
What a giant splash you make
When you jump into the pool
To keep yourself both wet and cool.
Although you are so big and round
As you walk and shake the ground
But when you start to swim, I see,
You are as graceful as can be!

Language Experience

Make a vocabulary list for hippos. Some words to start off with are fat, wet, squatty, yawn.

Creative Dramatics

The children can walk slowly, lumbering like a hippo. Next do a big hippo yawn, and get in the river. Do a smooth hippo glide in the water.

Literature-Based Activity: Hot Box Hippo

Supplies: Pattern, one discarded hamburger box from a fast food restaurant, either cardboard or foam, glue, construction paper, tape, a pencil, and one plastic straw.

Directions: The front of the box, where it opens, will be the hippo's mouth. Use pattern to trace ears, eyes, teeth and nostrils onto the construction paper. Cut out and glue to the box. Use the pencil to poke a hole in the center of the bottom of the box. Push the straw halfway through the hole. Bend it and tape one end to the inside top of the box. Pushing and pulling on the straw will make the hippo's mouth open and close.
Cost per hippo: 8¢

❏ Additional Literature Selections

Arnold, Caroline. *Hippo*. Morrow, 1992.

Flanders, Micheal. *The Hippopotamus Song*. Little Brown, 1991.

Hiskey, Iris. *Hannah Hippo's No Mud Day*. Simon and Schuster, 1991.

Macarthy, Bobette. *Ten Little Hippos: A Counting Book*. Macmillan, 1992.

MacDonald, Mary Ann. *Little Hippo Starts School*. Dial, 1990.

Mahy, Margaret. *The Boy Who Was Followed Home*. Franklin Watts, 1975.

Martin, Bill. *The Happy Hippopotami*. Harcourt Brace Jovanovich, 1991.

Matsuoka, Kymoko. *There's a Hippo in My Bath*. Doubleday, 1989.

Parker, Nancy. *Love from Uncle Clyde*. Dodd, 1977.

Hippo Nametag

Hot Box Hippo

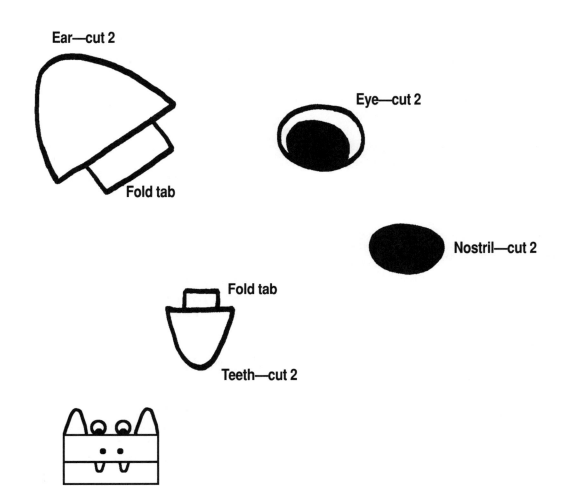

Ear—cut 2

Fold tab

Eye—cut 2

Nostril—cut 2

Fold tab

Teeth—cut 2

I is for *Invertebrate*

Invertebrates are animals that don't have a backbone. Sponges, jellyfish, coral, worms, starfish, insects, crayfish and spiders are all invertebrates.

Wonderful Worms

By Linda Glaser. (Millbrook Press, 1992)

This book describes the life, behavior, and characteristics of the earthworm as seen through the eyes of a boy. The life of a worm is contrasted and compared with that of a human being. Activities by boy and worm both above and below ground are depicted.

❏ Warm-Up Activities

Song

Wiggle Worms

(To the tune of "Row, Row, Row Your Boat")
Wiggle, wiggle, wiggle worms
Wiggling all around.
Wiggle here, wiggle there,
Wiggle in the ground.
Repeat with "Crawl, crawl, crawl," "Squirm, squirm, squirm," etc.
Wiggle fingers as you sing.

Also use the tape *Grandpa Art Sings Insect Songs* by Arthur Luster, Sun Group, 1992.

"Walter the Waltzing Worm" from *Walter the Waltzing Worm* by Hap Palmer, Educational Activities, Inc., 1982.

Fingerplay

1, 2, 3, There's a Bug on Me!

1, 2, 3, there's a bug on me!
(pretend to brush bug off)
Where did it go? I don't know!
(shrug shoulders)

❏ Follow-Up Activities

Poetry

Worm

What does he see
Under the ground?

Squirming and worming
Himself around...
Wriggling and wiggling
Along his way,
How can he tell
If it's night or day?

Under a Rock

I picked up a rock
I saw a worm
I watched him wiggle,
Squiggle,
Squirm.
Hello, worm!
How are you today?
But the worm just
Wiggle,
Squiggle,
Squirmed away!

Language Experience

Make a wormy vocabulary list for the kids. They can include worm words such as wiggle, squiggle, squirm, etc.

Creative Dramatics

Children can act out worm movements such as wiggle, squirm, squiggle. Use the word list you made from the language experience above. Recite the following rhyme:

Worms are crawling, crawling, crawling,
Worms are crawling all around.
Wiggly worms are squiggly, squiggly,
Squirming on the ground.

Literature-Based Activities: Wiggle Worms

Supplies: One 3" circle of brown construction paper, scissors, a pencil, a 16" piece of brown yarn, a brown crayon, and uncooked macaroni.

Directions: Take the circle of paper and punch a hole in the center with the point of the pencil. Slide it on to the yarn. Tie off the end of the yarn so the circle will not come off. Draw facial features on the circle. Now thread the macaroni on the yarn until it is filled up. Tie off the other end of the yarn so the macaroni will not come off. The ends of the worm can be tied together and worn as a necklace.
Cost per worm: 17¢

Worm Watch

Supplies: You will need two different kinds of earthworms, some shallow pans and soil.
Directions: Fill the pans with soil and add a few worms to each. Have the children divide into small groups and give each group a pan. Discuss what the worms look like, and record the children's comments about what the worms do.

Worm Painting

Supplies: Yarn and a little paint.
Directions: Dip the yarn in paint and wiggle on paper as a worm would. Let it dry and display.

For information on worms and composting, contact:
The Worm Concern, 1-805-496-2872.

To obtain live insects for observation, contact:
Insect Lore Products
PO Box 1535
Shafter, CA 93263
1-800-LIVE BUG; or

Flowerfield Enterprises, 10332 Shaver Road, Kalamazoo, Michigan, 49002, (616) 327-0180.

❏ Additional Literature Selections

Berger, Melvin. *Stranger Than Fiction: Killer Bugs.* Avon Books, 1990.

Eyewitness Explorers: Insects. Dorling Kindersley, 1992.

Falkham, Margery. *The Big Bug Book,* Little Brown, 1994.

Hemsley, William. *Jellyfish to Insects.* Gloucester, 1990.

Henwood, Chris. *Earthworms.* Franklin Watts, 1988.

Hopkins, Lee Bennett, comp. *Flit, Flutter, Fly: Poems About Bugs and Other Crawly Creatures.* Doubleday, 1992.

Jeunesse, Gallimard. *The Ladybug and Other Insects.* Scholastic, 1991.

"Little Bug, Little Bug," p. 56-57, from *Paper Stories* by Jean Stangl, David S. Lake Publishers, 1984.

McKissack, Patricia. *Bugs!* Children's Press, 1988.

Ryder, Joanne. *When the Woods Hum.* William Morrow, 1991.

"W," p. 68-70 from *Paper-Cutting Stories from A to Z* by Valerie Marsh, Alleyside Press, 1992.

Ziefert, Harriet. *Worm Day.* Little Brown, 1987.

Invertebrate Nametag

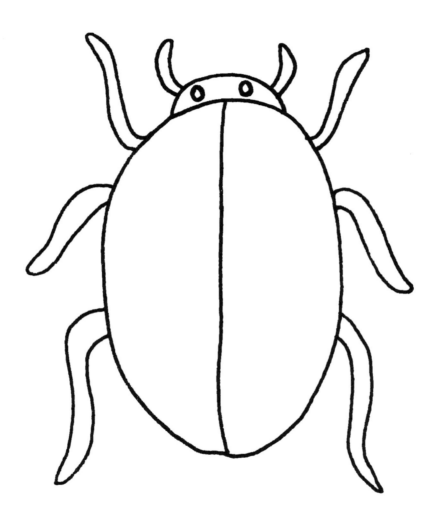

# J is for *Jack-o'-lantern*

Make jack-o'-lantern chains to decorate. Draw a pump-kin on a strip of orange paper, fold it accordion-style with sides of the pumpkin touching the folds. Cut, leaving the folds intact. Decorate and drape your area.

The Little Old Lady Who Was Not Afraid of Anything

By Linda Williams. (Crowell, 1986)

A brave, little old lady is followed by gloves, a hat, shoes and other objects trying to scare her. The last thing she meets is a jack-o'-lantern who says *Boo! Boo!* and succeeds in scaring her for a minute. Later, she talks the objects into being a scarecrow.

❏ Warm-Up Activities

Fingerplay

I am a Pumpkin

I am a pumpkin, big and round
(use arms to make a circle)
Once upon a time I grew on the ground.
(point to the ground)
Now I have a mouth, two eyes, and a nose.
(point to features on your face)
What are they for, do you suppose?
(shrug shoulders)
When I have a candle inside shining bright,
(hold up index finger)
I'll be a jack-o'-lantern on Halloween night!
(place hands on face and peek through fingers)

Rhyme

See my jack-o'-lantern round and fat;
With its candle so yellow.
Watch his grin on Halloween night,
Because he is a funny fellow.

Song

The Great Pumpkin

(To the tune of "Here We Go Round the Mulberry Bush")
We're sitting in the pumpkin patch, waiting on the great pumpkin,

I think I see him in the sky, is that the pumpkin?
Oh it's just a _____, it's not the pumpkin.
So we'll stay right in the patch, where is the pumpkin!
Sing the song using the words "black cat," "funny bat," "white ghost," etc. It is also fun to make stick puppets of the different characters. Some of the children can walk through as you sing, while the rest of the seated children are pumpkins in the patch.

❏ Follow-Up Activities

Poetry

Who Am I?

They chose me from the patch
"That's the nicest one," they said.
And carved me out a face
Then put a candle in my head.
They set me on the doorstep
The night was dark and wild.
But when they lit the candle
Then I smiled.

Smiling Jack

I have a jack-o'-lantern
As round as can be,
I scoop out his seeds,
And cut eyes so he can see.
Next I cut a curving mouth...
He's smiling at me.

Language Experience

Use the story by Linda Williams to do a mapping project. As a group, draw the road, woods, the cottage, path, and then place all of the objects in the appropriate locations. Have the children label the objects and places on the map. Have them decide where the field and the location of the herbs and spices would be. Make a picture of the little old lady on a separate sheet that can be cut out and moved along the map as the story is read.

Creative Dramatics

This story is a participation story. Simply have the children do the movements and recite the noises as the story is read. For example, have them stand and stomp their feet on "Clomp! Clomp!"

Have a pumpkin race. This is similar to an old fashioned egg race. Give each player a spoon and several miniature pumpkins or orange balls. The pumpkins are carried from one spot to another on the spoons as quickly as possible.

Use the book *Mousekin's Golden House* to do some mime:
> seeds popping
> cat creeping
> owl swooping
> Mousekin jumping
> wind and snow blowing
> Mousekin sleeping.

Literature Based Activity:Winking Jack-o'-Lantern

Supplies: Pattern, sheet of orange paper, scissors, a small strip of white paper, a black crayon, and a green crayon.
Directions: Using pattern, cut out a pumpkin shape for each child. Draw eyes, nose and a mouth, and color in the nose and mouth with the black crayon. Be sure and draw the eyes no taller than the height of the strip of white paper. Cut out the eyes. Cut a slip on either side of the eyes the size of the strip. With the strip centered behind the eyes, draw pupils on the strip. Move the strip back and forth to make the eyes "wink."
Cost per jack-o'-lantern: 5¢

❏ Additional Literature Selections

Dillon, Jana. *Jeb Scarecrow's Pumpkin Patch.* Houghton Mifflin, 1992.

Friskey, Margaret. *The Perky Little Pumpkin.* Children's Press, 1990.

Gillis, Jennifer. *In a Pumpkin Shell.* Storey Communications, 1992.

Johnston, Tony. *The Vanishing Pumpkin.* Putnam, 1990.

McDonald, Megan. *The Great Pumpkin Switch.* Orchard, 1992.

Miller, Edna. *Mousekin's Golden House.* Prentice, 1964.

Ray, M.L. *Pumpkins.* Harcourt Brace Jovanovich, 1992.

Schultz, Charles. *It's the Great Pumpkin, Charlie Brown.* New American Library, 1967.

Ray, David. *Pumpkin Light.* Putnam and Grossett, 1993.

"Three Brave Hunters," p. 53-59, from *Cut and Tell Stories for Fall* by Jean Warren, Totline Press, 1990.

Titherington, Jeanne. *Pumpkin, Pumpkin.* Greenwillow, 1990.

Pumpkin Nametag

Winking Jack-o'-Lantern

 *is for* **Koala**

The koala is an Australian mammal that looks like a big teddy bear, but is not a bear at all. They are marsupials, which carry their babies in pouches.

Koala Lou

By Mem Fox. (Harcourt Brace Jovanovich, 1989)

Everyone loves little Koala Lou. Her mother tells her, "Koala Lou, I do love you," at least one hundred times a day. But too soon, other koala babies are born to Mother Koala. She forgets to tell Koala Lou that she loves her. Koala Lou is determined to recapture her mother's attention by winning the gum tree climbing event in the Bush Olympics. Detailed colored pencil illustrations help describe events.

❏ Warm-Up Activities

Fingerplays

Koala Bears

One little koala bear, finding things to do,
Along came another, and then there were two.
Two busy koala bears, climbing a eucalyptus tree,
Along came another, and then there were three.
Three lively koala bears who like to explore.
Along came another, and then there were four.
Four tired koala bears, ready for a nap,
They sleep in the trees, now what do you think of that?
(hold up 1, 2, 3, 4 fingers.)

Also "The Koala Hangs by His Claws on the Tree," from *The Zoo Comes to School*, p. 26.

Song

Silly Koala

Silly, silly koala bear!
Oh you gave us such a scare.
When you tried to climb the tree,
And almost fell on top of me!
Silly, silly koala bear.

❏ Follow-Up Activities

Poetry

Koala (An Acrostic Poem)

Koala
Ohh!
Adorable
Lovely
Australia

Koala Bear

Koala Bear, koala bear,
Climbing up a tree
Koala bear, koala bear
Eating eucalyptus leaves.
Koala bear, koala bear
With a joey on your back,
Koala bear, koala bear,
And a pocket like a sack.
Koala bear, koala bear,
You look so very small.
Koala bear, koala bear,
You're not a bear at all!

Language Experience

Using pattern, trace or copy one koala shape for each child. Let them color or draw in the features of the koala. As a class, compose a descriptive poem about koala bears. Introduce the children to some words to help, such as mammal, marsupial, Australia, eucalyptus, cubs and endangered.

Creative Dramatics

The children can do a little encyclopedia research on Australian animals. Before and after their research, have them act and make the noises they think each animal would do. Some animals to look up are: kangaroo, emu, possum, wombat, crocodile, bandicoot, echidna, dingo, kookaburra, platypus, and Tasmanian devil.

Literature-Based Activity: Paper Plate Koala Lou

Supplies: 6" paper plate, scissors, glue, a black crayon, a brown crayon, a pink crayon, a gray crayon, and scraps of gray paper.

Directions: Draw eyes, a nose, and a mouth on the paper plate. Color the eyes brown, the nose black, the mouth pink, and the rest of the plate gray. Cut two ear shapes out of the gray paper and glue to the paper plate.

Cost per koala: 6¢

❏ Additional Literature Selections

Arnold, Caroline. *Koala*. William Morrow, 1987.

Bassett, Lisa. *Koala's Christmas*. Cobblehill, 1991.

Gelman, Ruth. *A Koala Grows Up*. Scholastic, 1986.

Lepthien, Emilie. *Koalas*. Children's Press, 1990.

Nogure, Susan and Tony Chen. *Little Koala*. Random House, 1979.

Quackenbush, Robert. *I Don't Want to Go, I Don't Know How to Act*. Lippincott, 1983.

Stone, Lynn. *Koalas*. Rourke, 1990.

Trinca, Rod. *One Woolly Wombat*. Kane Miller, 1987.

Tripp, Valerie. *Baby Koala Finds a Home*. Children's Press, 1987.

"Why Koala Has No Tail," p. 74-80, from *Look Back and See* by Margaret Read MacDonald. HW Wilson, 1991.

Koala Nametag

Paper Plate Koala Lou

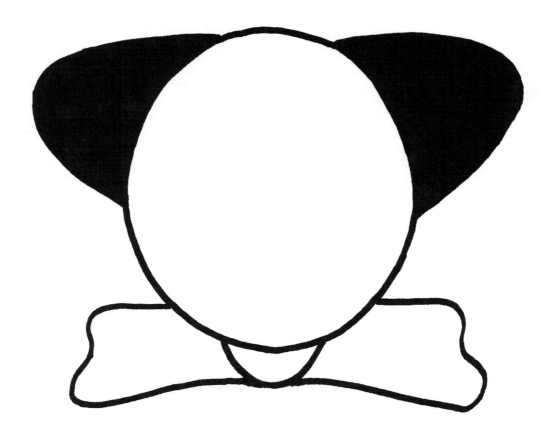

L is for Llama

The llama is a member of the camel family from South America. Llamas make good pets—they can survive just eating grass, are easy to train and friendly.

Llama and the Great Flood

By Ellen Alexander. (Thomas Y. Crowell, 1989)

In the Andes mountains of Peru, a llama has a bad dream that might come true. The llama tells his owner this news, and he leads all the animals to the top of Willka Qutu, the highest mountain peak. A colorful retelling of the Great Flood myth.

❏ Warm-Up Activities

Rhyme

I have a little llama
She is very nice and plump
And she always nuzzles me
For a sugar lump.

Song

"The Mama Llama Rock," by Derrie Frost, from *Zippity Zoo Day*, Melody House Music, 1989.

"I Have a Llama"

(To the tune of "Bingo")
I have a friend
Who has soft fur
And Llama is her name-o,
L-l-a-m-a, l-l-a-m-a, l-l-a-m-a,
And Llama is her name-o.

❏ Follow-Up Activities

Poetry

A llama has a
*Lll*ong, *lll*ong neck,
And very lovely eyes.
A llama seems so sweet and calm,
So it comes as a surprise,
That when a llama is upset,
or feeling rather blue,
She will chew and aim,
The spit
Right at you!

Language Experience

Use the book *Camel* to compare and contrast a llama and its relatives. Pictured on page 16 are a llama, camel, vicuna, alpaca, and guanaco.

Creative Dramatics

Dramatize these two poems:
"A is for Alpaca," from *Laughing Time* by W.J. Smith, Delacorte, 1980.
and
"The Llama Who Had No Pajama," from *Yellow Butter Purple Jelly Red Jam Black Bread* , by Mary Ann Hoberman, Viking 1981.

Literature-Based Activity: Folded Llama

Supplies: Pattern, scissors, and crayons.
Directions: Trace pattern copies onto heavy paper. Color llamas in different colors and patterns. Have children cut the patterns on the solid lines and fold the pattern as indicated.

For more information on llamas, write to:
International Llama Association
2755 S. Locust Street, #114
Denver, CO 80222.

❏ Additional Literature Selections

Arnold, Caroline. *Camel*. Morrow, 1992.

Arnold, Caroline. *Llama*. Morrow, 1988.

Bare, Colleen. *Love a Llama*. Dutton, 1994.

Cosgrove, Stephen. *Pish-Posh*. Price Stern, 1986.

Guarino, Deborah. *Is Your Mama a Llama?* Scholastic, 1991.

Hurwitz, Johanna. *A Llama in the Family*. Morrow, 1994.

Jones, Susan. *Llamas: Woolly, Winsome, and Wonderful*. Publishing Horizons, 1987. (PO Box 1038, Dublin, Ohio, 43017.)

LaBonte, Gail. *The Llama*. Dillon, 1989.

Palacioos, Afgentina. *Llama's Secret: A Peruvian Legend*. Troll, 1993.

Rockwell, Anne. *The Good Llama*. World, 1963.

"The Tale of the Gentle Folk," p. 95-101, from *Tales from Silver Lands* by Charles Finger, Doubleday, 1924.

Topooco, Eusebio. *Waira's First Journey*. Lothrop, Lee, and Shepherd, 1993.

Llama Nametag

Folded Llama

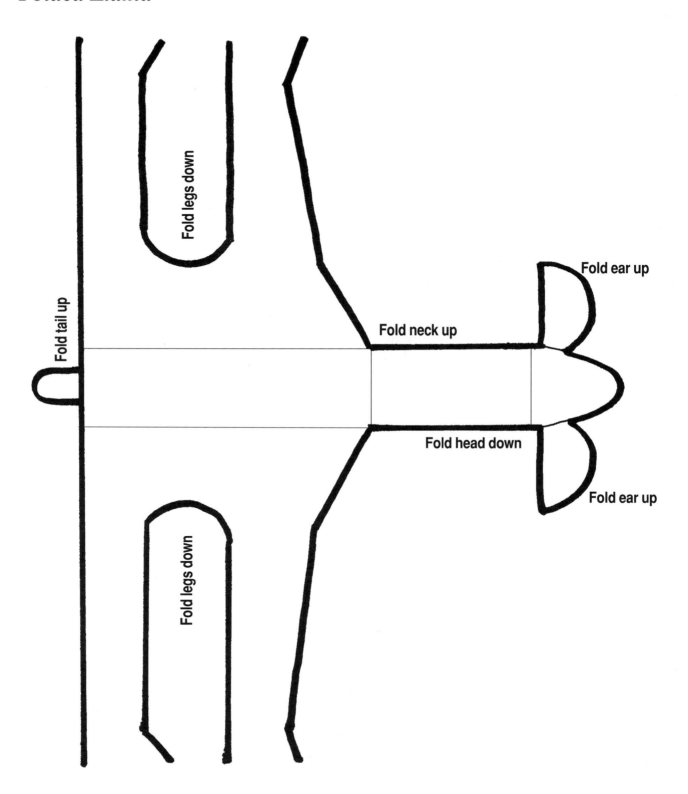

 **M** *is for* **Mice**

A tiny new born mouse weighs less than a penny. It is bald and pink, and its eyes are closed.

Ten Little Mice

By Joyce Dunbar. (Harcourt Brace Jovanovich, 1990)

A beautifully illustrated book of simple verse about the activities of a group of ten mice. One by one, each mouse tires of the days adventures and scurries home to the burrow. At last, all ten mice are safely home.

❏ Warm-Up Activities

Fingerplay

Five Little Mice *(Traditional)*

One little mouse
(hold up one finger)
Rocking in a tree,
(rocking motion with arms)
Two little mice
(hold up two fingers)
Splashing in the sea.
(splashing motion)
Three little mice
(three fingers)
Crawling on the floor,
(crawling motion)
Four little mice
(four fingers)
Scratching at the door.
(Scratching motion)
Five little mice
(five fingers)
Playing hide and seek,
(cover eyes)
Keep their eyes closed
'Till I say *Peek!*
(peek through fingers)

Song/Music

"Hickory Dickory Dock" from *Wee Sing: Children's Songs and Fingerplays* by Pamela Beall and Susan Nipp, Price Stern Sloan, 1979, p.11 (cassette and book).

❏ Follow-Up Activities

Poetry

Mouse

I once knew a tiny mouse
Who lived so quietly in my house.
My cat did not like him, he ate up all our cheese.
But I still asked my mother, "Can I keep him, *Please?*"

"The City Mouse and the Garden Mouse" by Christina Rossetti from *A Child's First Book of Poems*, Western Publishing, 1981, p. 35.

The City Mouse and the Garden Mouse

The city mouse lives in a house;
The garden mouse lives in a bower,
He's friendly with the frogs and toads,
And sees pretty plants in flower.
The city mouse eats bread and cheese;
The garden mouse eats what he can;
We will not grudge him seeds and stocks,
Poor little timid furry man.

Language Experience

Ask the children the following questions and record their answers on a piece of tagboard:

> What other animal might frighten a mouse to scurry home?

> What other reason can you think of for a mouse to go home to his nest?

Creative Dramatics

After making the "Ear All About It" mice ears in the Literature-Based Activities, choose children to pantomime the actions of the mice in *Ten Little Mice.*

Ten of the children can be the mice. If your group is large, you can also hang signs around the children's necks that let them be the following from the story:

robin	bees
cat	sheep
badger	owl

If your group is very large, make several signs that say sheep and bees.

Literature-Based Activity: "Ear All About It" Mouse Ears

Supplies: Pattern, 8½" x 11" brown construction paper, one 8½" x 11" pink construction paper and yarn. You will also need glue, scissors, a hole punch.
Directions: Draw patterns twice on brown and pink paper. Cut out the patterns. Glue the inner ear to the outer ear, and let dry flat. Punch two holes ½ " from the base of each ear at the "Xs." Thread yarn through the holes and tie on to child's head.
Cost per set of ears: 7¢ each

❏ Additional Literature Selections

Baker, Alan. *Two Tiny Mice*. Dial, 1990.

Cauley, Lorinda. *Three Blind Mice*. Putnam, 1991.

Fisher, Eileen. *The House of a Mouse*. Harper and Row, 1988.

Fleming, Denise. *Lunch*. Henry Holt, 1992.

Henkes, Kevin. *Owen*. Greenwillow, 1993.

Henrietta. *A Mouse in the House*. Dorling Kindersley, 1991.

Kraus, Robert. *Whose Mouse Are You?* Macmillan, 1970.

Sierra, Judy. "The Rat's Daughter: A Japanese Tale" from *The Flannel Board Storytelling Book*, H.W. Wilson, 1987, p. 128-133.

Stangl, Jean. "Two Scared Mice" from *Paper Stories*, David S. Lake Publishers, 1984, 77-79.

Walsh, Ellen. *Mouse Count*. Harcourt Brace Jovanovich, 1991.

Mouse Nametag

Mouse Ears

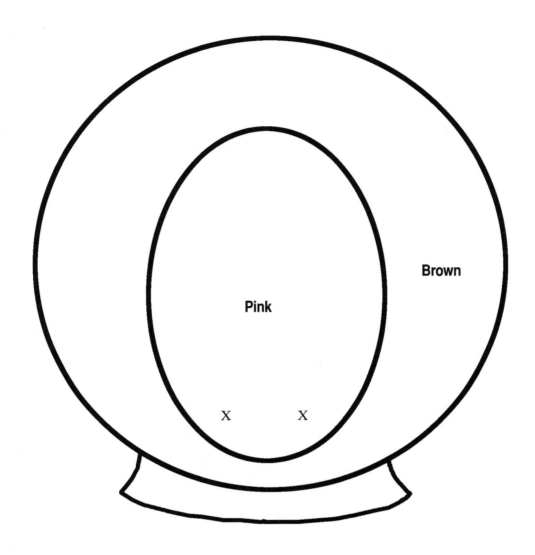

Brown

Pink

X   X

 *is for* **Night**

Look up at the stars	All of the stars
So many to see!	Over my head
So many stars	Shine so softly
But only one me.	As I go to bed.

Can't You Sleep, Little Bear?

By Martin Waddell. (Candlewick Press, 1988)

A charming tale of Big Bear and Little Bear, who has trouble sleeping. There is too much dark for Little Bear, so Big Bear tries to help him overcome his fears. Delicate watercolors by Barbara Firth convey this loving story and its happy ending.

❏ Warm-Up Activities

Fingerplay

The Tiny Stars

The tiny stars you see at night,
(point upward)
Are like the sun, so warm and bright.
(shade eyes)
But far away they look so small,
(separate thumb and index finger a small amount)
They barely give us light at all.
(shrug shoulders)

The Falling Star

I looked up at the dark night sky
(look up)
And saw a falling star pass by,
(point and move arm in an arc)
It went out before it hit the ground
(wiggle fingers then stop)
And to this day it can't be found.
(shade eyes and look around as if searching)

❏ Follow-Up Activities

Poetry

Night Song

Hush, hush, child
The sun is in the west.

The lamb in the meadow
Has lain down to rest.
The bough rocks the birch,
The flower rocks the bee,
The wave rocks the fish,
The wind rocks the tree.
So rock at night
So softly to sleep
Do not wake up
Until the birds peep.

Language Experience

Sometimes spontaneous writing by children can be as lovely as poetry. On a large sheet of paper, write the words "A star is..."

Let the children dictate words and descriptions of what a star is to them. Write their responses and post for all to see.

Creative Dramatics

For this project you can use two teddy bears, a chair, a book, a flashlight, one paper moon and as many paper stars as you need. The story *Can't You Sleep, Little Bear?* has lots of dialogue, and lends itself well to making a playlet. Children can read or improvise the main idea of the story. One child can be Big Bear, one child can be Little Bear, and the rest are the moon and stars. Practice and present to parents if possible.

Literature-Based Activity: Glitter Stars

Each child can have their own star to take as a reminder of the story. The glitter stars take two days to dry, so they should be made in advance.
Supplies: You will need white glue, glitter, and wax paper.
Directions: For each star, draw a star outline with the white glue on the wax paper. Make the glue outline very thick. Completely cover the glue with glitter and let dry for two days. Pour off the excess glitter and

save it. Very carefully peel the stars off the wax paper from each point inward.
Cost per star: $1.40

❏ Additional Literature Selections

Berger, Barbara. *Grandfather Twilight*. Putnam, 1986.

Birdseye, Tom. *A Song of Stars*. Holiday House, 1990.

Butler, Daphne. *A First Look at Day and Night*. Gareth Stevens, 1991.

Greenfield, Eloise. *Night on Neighborhood Street*. Dial, 1991.

Hong, Lilly Toy. *How the Ox Star Fell from Heaven*. Alfred A. Whitman, 1991.

I See the Moon: Goodnight Lullabies and Poems. North South Books, 1991.

Lee, Jeannie M. *The Legend of the Milky Way*. Holt, 1982.

Montgomery, Micheal. *'Night America*. Contemporary Books, 1989.

Zimelman, Nathan. *The Star of Melvin*. Macmillan, 1987.

Night Nametag

 *is for* **Octopus**

Cover paper plates with blue cellophane. Attach eight strips of cellophane around the edge with tape. Hang these beautiful octopi and green crepe paper from the ceiling to create an underwater atmosphere.

Down in the Sea: The Octopus
By Patricia Kite. (Albert Whitman, 1993)

This book describes the physical characteristics, habitat, and food of the octopus. Illustrated with high-quality, full-color photographs. Many unusual and little known facts about this creature are included.

❏ Warm-Up Activities

Fingerplay

Little Octopus

See the little octopus,
(wiggle eight fingers)
Swimming in the sea.
(move fingers back and forth)
Wiggle, wiggle go his legs
(wiggle fingers again)
As he swims by me.
(point to self)
I jump in the water
(jump up)
And what do you suppose?
That squiggly, wiggly octopus
(wiggle eight fingers)
And I are nose to nose!
(point to nose)

Other Fingerplays

"The Octopus Swims, His Many Arms Free," from *The Zoo Comes to School*, p. 31.

"I Wish I Were an Octopus," by Helen Fletcher from *Fingerplay Poems and Stories*, Teacher's Publishing, 1958, p. 25. (O.P.)

❏ Follow-Up Activities

Poetry

The Octopus

Here's something
To make you think—
The octopus
Can squirt black ink.
But he can't write—
He has no pen.
He can count to eight,
But never ten.

Eight Arms

With eight arms
Swim in the ocean
Tentacles making
A big commotion,
Who has so many feet?
An octopus—they help him eat.

Language Experience

After sharing *Down in the Sea*, have the children dictate a pet care style story about having an octopus. Be sure to include where the octopus would sleep, what he would eat, how he would exercise, and some good octopus names.

To do some real research about octopus, use the book *Tentacles: The Amazing World of Octopus, Squid, and Their Relatives* by James Martin, Crown, 1993.

Creative Dramatics

Have the children imagine all the things they could do better or more of if they had eight arms. After making a list, go through and have each child act out one of the ideas.

Literature-Based Activity: Handy Octopus

Supplies: One sheet of 8½" x 11" sheet of green construction paper, one sheet of 8½" x 11" sheet of blue construction paper, scissors, glue, and a black crayon.

Directions: Have the children fold their thumbs up and place both hands next to each other on top of the green paper. Trace around the outside of the eight fingers with the crayon. The children can take turns tracing each others hands. Next, cut out the octopus shape. Draw a face as shown in the Octopus pattern. (Cereal "O's" could also be glued to the arms to show the suction cups.) Glue the octopus shape to the blue paper. A large mural can be made using a sheet of blue butcher paper or poster board with crepe paper streamers for seaweed.

Cost per octopus: 7¢

❏ Additional Literature Selections

Brandenburg, Franz. *Otto Is Different*. Greenwillow, 1985.

Carrick, Carol. *Octopus*. Seabury Press, 1978.

Heller, Ruth. *How to Hide an Octopus*. Grossett and Dunlap, 1985.

Kraus, Robert. *Herman the Helper*. Dutton, 1981.

Lauber, Patricia. *An Octopus Is Amazing*. Harper, 1990.

Most, Bernard. *My Very Own Octopus*. Harcourt Brace Jovanovich, 1991.

Schultz, Ellen. *I Can Read About the Octopus*. Troll, 1979.

Ungerer, Tomi. *Emile*. Harper and Brothers, 1960.

Octopus Nametag

Handy Octopus

P is for Plant

Make leaf chains: Gather fallen leaves with long stems. Take two leaves and remove the stem of one. Overlap the tip of one leaf with the base of the other and use the stem like a straight pin to "pin" the leaves together.

Red Leaf, Yellow Leaf
By Lois Ehlert. (Harcourt Brace Jovanovich, 1991)

A child describes the growth of a maple tree from seed to sapling. Interesting collage pictures that include real leaves and branches illustrate the words. A useful plant care and bird feeding guide is included in the back.

❏ Warm-Up Activities

Fingerplay

Leaves

Five little leaves fluttered in the breeze,
Tumbled and fell down off the trees.
The first leaf said, "I am red."
And fell into a flower bed.
The second one, orange, said,
"Pick me up before I get wet."
The third little leaf said,
"I am yellow,
I look just like a canary fellow."
The fourth leaf said, "Well, I'm green,
The prettiest green you have ever seen."
The fifth leaf said, "I am brown,
And I will blow all over town."
(hold up 1, 2, 3, 4, and 5 fingers.)

Song

Leaves Fall Down

(To the tune of "Here We Go Round the Mulberry Bush")
The leaves are turning yellow and red, yellow and red, yellow and red,
The leaves are turning yellow and red, on a beautiful morning.
The leaves are falling down to the ground, down to the ground, down to the ground,
The leaves are falling down tot he ground,
On a beautiful morning.

❏ Follow-Up Activities

Poetry

Flower Garden

A flower garden
It's planting time!
Out comes the sun
See it shine?
The seeds start to grow
And after a shower
The little seed
Is now a flower.

Language Experience

Have the children collect a variety of leaves, grasses, and flowers from home. Press them flat. Directions for making a plant press can be found on page 98 of *Adventures in Art: Art and Craft Experiences for 7 to 14 Year Olds* by Susan Milord, Williamson Publishing, 1990. Mount the leaves on construction paper with a dab of glue. Try to identify the species, and let the children label them.

Another idea is to have the children illustrate some special plants, such as money plant, kissing plant, crying flower, etc. Let them dictate a story about one of these imaginary plants after they draw.

Creative Dramatics

Find pictures of a seed growing into a plant. Show them and explain the process to the children. Have the children curl up into a seed shape, be planted, grow into a seedling. Tell them to wilt from lack of water, then perk back up. Tell them to grow and grow into tall trees.

Use the book of creative drama about plants *Tick Tock, The Popcorn Clock* by Jane Moncure, Children's Press, 1978.

Literature-Based Activity: Paper Garden

This is a very simple, yet creative project.
Supplies: You will need a 4' length of green butcher paper, old seed catalogs or magazines with plants, vegetables and flowers, glue.
Directions: Lay the butcher paper on the floor. Have children go through the catalogs and magazines for pictures of plants they like. The children will then arrange and glue them to the butcher paper to form an imaginary garden.
Cost: 3¢ per child

Mini Terrarium

You will need one large plastic soft drink bottle, a spoon, one cup potting soil, grass seeds, water.

Spoon the potting soil into the soft drink bottle until there are 4"on the bottom. Sprinkle grass seed into the bottle. Shake the bottle so the seeds and soil mix a little. Add a few spoonfuls of water to the soil. Place the bottle by a window and keep it moist. In about ten days you will have a mini terrarium.

For a free newsletter, ideas and other information, write to:
National Gardening Association
Education Department
180 Flynn Avenue
Burlington, VT 05401
or
For seeds, write to:
Burgess Seeds
Box 3000
Galesburg, MI 49053

Burpee Seeds
300 Park Avenue
Warminister, Pennsylvania 18974

❏ Additional Literature Selections

Carle, Eric. *The Tiny Seed*. Picture Book Studio, 1987.

Ehlert, Lois. *Planting a Rainbow*. Harcourt Brace Jovanovich, 1988.

Gibbons, Gail. *From Seed to Plant*. Holiday House, 1991.

Grover, Max. *The Zucchini Alphabet*. Harcourt, 1993.

Hutchins, Pat. *Titch*. Macmillan, 1979.

Ichikawa, Satomi. *Rosy's Garden*. Philomel, 1990.

Kellogg, Stephen. *Jack and the Beanstalk*. Morrow, 1991.

Lauber, Patricia. *Seeds: Pop, Stick, and Glide*. Crown, 1988.

Lester, Helen. *Pookins Gets Her Way*. Houghton Mifflin, 1987.

"Really Spring," p. 67-70, from *Chalk in Hand: The Draw and Tell Book* by Phyllis Noe Pflomm, Scarecrow, 1986.

Robson, Denny. *Grow It for Fun*. Gloucester, 1991.

Walker, Lois. *Get Growing!* John Wiley and Sons, 1990.

Plant Nametag

 *is for* **Quill**

A porcupine is a rodent with long prickly quills. Watch out—when a porcupine is threatened, it can erect its sharp quills—but it can't shoot them!

A Porcupine Named Fluffy
By Helen Lester. (Houghton Mifflin, 1986)

When Mr. and Mrs. Porcupine have a baby, they name him, of all things, Fluffy. Try as he might, the porcupine child is just not Fluffy. And so Fluffy tries a number of ways to be fluffy, but remains unsatisfied with his name. Until he meets a grumbly rhinoceros named Hippo.

❏ Warm-Up Activities

Fingerplay

Porcupines

Five little porcupines underneath a tree.
The first one said, "What do I see?"
The second one said, "Some plants on the ground."
The third one said, "Those are plants I found."
The fourth one said, "I'll race you there."
The fifth one said, "All right, that's fair."
So they raised their quills and waddled with glee,
And ate the plants and the bark off the tree.

Song

"Porcupine" from *Animal Alphabet Songs* by David S. Polansky, Perfect Score Music, 1982.

Oh, Porcupine
(Sung to the tune of "Oh, Christmas Tree")
Oh, porcupine, oh, porcupine,
How prickly are your quills.
Oh, porcupine, oh porcupine,
How prickly are your quills.
Although you're nice and brownish black,
You're like a pincushion on your back.
Oh, porcupine, oh, porcupine,
How prickly are your quills.

❏ Follow-Up Activities

Poetry

The Porcupine

The bears have fur to keep them warm.
The birds have feathers to brave the storm.
But what good are prickly pins
When the snow or rain begins?
A dog,
A cat,
Are nice to pat.
Even though they are friendly folk
Porcupines are not nice to stroke!

Language Experience

The porcupine is such a unique animal that it is perfect as the subject of descriptive poetry. Write a poem as a group with the children free associating words such as prickly, spiky, slow, etc. that describe this unusual rodent.

Creative Dramatics

After sharing the book *A Porcupine Named Fluffy*, have the children try to act out the word "fluffy." Next, try "prickly" and other textural words.

Literature-Based Activity: Paper Plate Porcupine

Supplies: One half of a 6" paper plate, glue, a straw cut into 1" sections, scraps of brown construction paper, scissors, and crayons. See pattern for guidance.
Directions: Glue the straw sections along the curved edge of the paper plate. These are the quills. Color the plate if desired, and draw facial features on it. Cut two half circles from the brown paper scraps and glue to the straight edge of the plate to serve as feet.
Cost per porcupine: 9¢

❏ Additional Literature Selections

Annett, Cora. *When Porcupine Moved In*. Franklin
   Watts, 1971.

Christian, Mary B. *Penrod's Party*. Macmillan, 1990.

Dalmais, Anne-Marie. *Mr. Porcupine's Marvelous
   Flying Machine*. Golden Press, 1972.

Green, Carl. *The Porcupine*. Crestwood House, 1985.

Harshman, Terry. *Porcupine's Pajama Party*. Harper
   and Row, 1988.

Major, Beverly. *Porcupine Stew*. Morrow, 1982.

Morgan, Mary. *Benjamin's Bugs*. Macmillan,

1994.

Quill Nametag

Paper Plate Porcupine

R is for *Rattlesnake*

Rattlesnake's slither
Makes me shiver,
Rattlesnake's slide
Makes me hide!

The Cactus Flower Bakery

By Harry Allard. (HarperCollins, 1991)

Sunny is a lovely rattlesnake who lives alone in the desert because all the other animals are afraid of her. Then Sunny meets Stuart, a nearsighted armadillo. She shares her homemade cakes, pies, and macaroons with him. Together, the two friends open The Cactus Flower Bakery, which is a huge success.

❑ Warm-Up Activities

Fingerplay

Wiggly, wiggly, wiggly snake
Is crawling all around.
Slithery, slippery, flippery snake,
Wiggles across the ground.

Rhyme

Rattlesnake

The sneaky slithery slippery snake
Slid through the grasses
Making them shake.
He's not a snake I want to see,
Oh, no! He's rattling at me!

Song

Baby Rattlesnake

(To the tune of "I'm Bringing Home a Baby Bumble Bee.")
I'm bringing home a baby rattlesnake,
Won't my mommy jump into the lake?
I'm bringing home a baby rattlesnake,
Sss, sss, sss, sss, sss!

Song

(To the tune of "I'm Being Eaten By a Boa Constrictor," from Where the Sidewalk Ends, *by Shel Silverstein, Columbia Records, 1984.)*

I'm being chased by a runaway rattler, a runaway rattler, a runaway rattler.
I'm being eaten by a runaway rattler,
And I don't like it very much.
Oh, no,
Here he comes.
Oh, no, he's after me.
Oh, yes, I'm going to flee.
Oh, no, he won't catch me!

❑ Follow-Up Activities

Poetry

In the desert
When the days are hot,
The rattlesnake
Finds a sunny spot.
He hardly moves
A bit.
He sits
And sits
And sits
And sits.

Language Experience

Share the poem "Rattlesnake Skipping Song," by Dennis Lee from *The Poetry Troupe*, I. Wilner, ed., Scribner, 1977.

Creative Dramatics

Have the children lie carefully on a clean area of the floor, on blankets or carpet. Let them practice slithering in place, and recite this rhyme:

Here's a rattlesnake
Crawling to me
A long, thin, wiggly
Rattlesnake I see—*Aaaaaaahhhhh!*

Literature-Based Activity: Sunny the Rattler

Supplies: Pattern, one empty egg carton, yarn, scissors, tape, a 3" x 3" square of construction paper, popcorn or dried beans, and crayons.

Directions: Using the scissors, cut off the bottoms of all the egg cups from the egg carton. Poke a hole in the center of each cup bottom. Tie a knot in one end of the yarn. Now string the remaining egg cups on the yarn, tying a knot after each cup to keep it in place. Cut a rattler using pattern and fold on the dotted lined. Put a few of the popcorn seeds or beans in the center of the tail and tape it shut. Tape to the end of the yarn with the small end pointing out. Use paper scraps to make a forked tongue. Decorate with crayons.

❏ Additional Literature Selections

Ata, Te and Lynn Moroney. *Baby Rattlesnake.* Children's Book Press, 1989.

Baker, Keith. *Hide and Snake.* Harcourt Brace Jovanovich, 1991.

Bargar, Sherie. *Rattlesnakes.* Rourke, 1986.

Dewey, Ariane. *The Narrow Escapes of Davy Crockett...* Greenwillow, 1990.

Freedman, Russell. *Rattlesnakes.* Holiday House, 1984.

Hall, Katy. *Snakey Riddles.* Dial, 1990.

Lee, Sandra. *Rattlesnakes.* Children's World, 1992.

Reed, Lynn. *Rattlesnake Stew.* Farrar, Strauss, and Giroux, 1990.

Reese, Bob. *Rapid Robert and Hiss the Snake.* Children's Press, 1983.

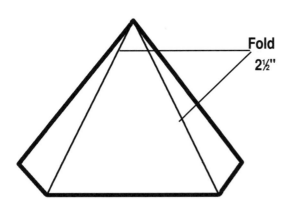

Fold
2½"

Sunny the Rattler

Rattlesnake Nametag

 *is for* **Sheep**

Sheep are very useful animals. They provide milk to make cheese, fine wool, meat, leather goods!

Borreguita and the Coyote
By Verna Aardema. (Knopf, 1991)

Borreguita is a sweet little sheep who is threatened by a hungry coyote, but escapes being eaten through trickery. End papers have imaginative Mexican-inspired designs and illustrations reminiscent of Diego Rivera.

❏ Warm-Up Activities

Chant

Five Little Sheep

Five little sheep, lying in the grass
Along came the shepherd, down the garden path.
He took a little sheep through the garden door,
Goodbye, sheep! Now there are four.
Four little sheep, lying in the grass
Along came the shepherd, down the garden path.
He led a little sheep down to the sea,
Goodbye, sheep! Now there are three.
Three little sheep, lying in the grass
Along came the shepherd, down the garden path.
He led a little sheep to it's mother ewe.
Goodbye, sheep! Now there are two.
Two little sheep, lying in the grass
Along can the shepherd, down the garden path.
He led a little sheep for a lovely run,
Goodbye, sheep! Now there is one.
One little sheep lying in the grass
Along came the shepherd, down the garden path.
He led a little sheep into the evening sun,
Goodbye, sheep! Now there are none.

Fingerplay

This is the White Sheep

This is the white sheep,
(left hand is sheep, right hand is shears)
And this is the way
The farmer cuts off the wool one day.

The wool was spun into thread so fine.
And made into cloth for this coat of mine.
(point to self)

Song

"Baa Baaa Black Sheep," from *Singable Songs for the Very Young* by Raffi, ShoreLine A & M Records, 1976.

❏ Follow-Up Activities

Poetry

Counting Sheep

Sometimes at night I cannot sleep,
I pass the time counting sheep.
The sheep are fluffy, black or white,
As I count them through the night.
I count and count all night long
And listen to their sheepy song.
Who would have guessed the noise they make,
My counting sheep keep me awake!

Language Experience

See pattern for "Sheep Shapes." Children can write a descriptive poem about sheep on the shapes, or color the shapes. Compose a poem made up of words that the children are reminded of when they think of sheep, such as, soft, wooly, white, etc.

Creative Dramatics

Using some of the many sounds from the story, have the children repeat them while pantomiming an action to go with them. For example, Borreguita says, "*Baa-a-a-a, Baa-a-a-a!*"; The coyote says, "*Grrr!*"; the water goes, "*Shuh, shuh, shuh, shuh*"; the coyote howls, "*Owoooooah!*"

Literature-Based Activity: Cottony Borreguita Puppet

Supplies: Pattern (for reference), one 8½" x 11" piece of white paper, a black crayon, 8 cotton balls, glue, scissors, tape, and a popsicle stick.

Directions: Trace a child's hand on the white paper with the thumb and pinky extended and three middle fingers together. Glue 4 cotton balls on the pinky and 4 cotton balls on the thumb of the cutout. These are the sheep's ears. Draw features on the sheep, then tape it to the popsicle stick. These Borreguita puppets can be used with the creative drama activity above. (See Collony Borreguita pattern)

Cost per sheep: 7¢

❏ Additional Literature Selections

Brenner, Barbara. *Ups and Downs With Lion and Lamb*. Bantam, 1991.

Bursik, Rose. *Zoe's Sheep*. Henry Holt, 1994.

Clayton, Gordon. *Lamb*. Dutton, 1992.

Crampton, Patricia. *My Little Lamb*. Bradbury, 1987.

DePaola, Tomie. *Charlie Needs a Cloak*. Prentice Hall, 1974.

Keller, Holly. *Ten Sleepy Sheep*. Greenwillow, 1983.

Levine, Arthur. *Sheep Dreams*. Dial, 1993.

Lewis, Kim. *The Shepherd Boy*. Four Winds, 1990.

Novak, Matt. *While the Shepherd Slept*. Orchard, 1991.

Shaw, Nancy. *Sheep in a Shop*. Houghton Mifflin, 1991.

Wallace, Barbara. *Argyle*. Abingdon, 1987.

Wellington, Monica. *Sheep Follow*. Dutton, 1992.

Sheep Nametag

Sheep Shape

Cottony Borreguita Puppet

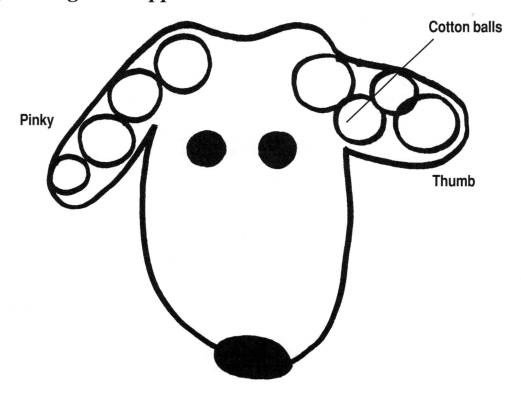

T is for Turkey

When most of us think of a turkey, we think of a delicious, golden brown bird on the Thanksgiving table. But the turkey is also the bird that Ben Franklin thought was more noble than the eagle!

A Turkey for Thanksgiving
By Eve Bunting. (Clarion, 1991)

Mrs. Moose wishes that they had turkey for Thanksgiving, so Mr. Moose sets off to find one. He and his friends rabbit, porcupine, sheep and goat all join in the search. The poor turkey runs away, not realizing the Moose want him as a guest, not dinner.

❑ Warm-Up Activities

Fingerplay

Five Little Turkeys

Five little turkeys sitting in a tree
Said the first little turkey, "What do I see?"
Said the second little turkey, "A farmer with a gun!"
Said the third little turkey, "Away let's run!"
Said the fourth little turkey "I'm not afraid!"
Said the fifth little turkey, "Let's hide in the shade."
Then *Bang! Bang! Bang!* went the farmer's gun
And away, away did the turkeys run!
(hold up 5, 4, 3, 2, and 1 finger.)

Song

"Three Turkeys" by Lucille Wood from *Songs from Singing Fun*, Bowmar Publishing, 1966.

The night before Thanksgiving, when I had gone to bed,
I heard three turkey gobblers, and this is what they said.
The first turkey said, "I think that I will go,
And hide behind a haystack where no one will know."
The second turkey said, "I think I'll find a tree,
And hide up in the branches, where no one will see."
The third turkey said, "I think it would be fun,
To hide the farmer's hatchet, then run, run, run, run."
Then on Thanksgiving morning, when the farmer came around
Those three turkey gobblers could not be found.

Also "The Turkey Wobble" by Jill Galina from *Holiday Songs for All Occasions*, Kimbo Educational Records, 1978.

"Five Fat Turkeys" Flannel Board Song from *Flannel Board Fun*, p. 116-120, by Diane Briggs, Scarecrow, 1992.

❑ Follow-Up Activities

Poetry

"One Fat Turkey"
by Susan Olson Higgins

One Fat Turkey
One fat turkey went strutting by,
He shook his feathers and winked his eye.
He flapped his wings and his head gave a wobble,
As he looked at me and said, "Gobble, gobble, gobble!"

"Turkeys on Parade"
by Dick Burns

Turkeys on Parade
Here comes the brown turkey
Ruffle, ruffle, ruffle.
Here comes the red turkey
Fluff, fluff, fluff.
Here comes the orange turkey
Gobble, gobble, gobble.
Here come all the turkeys
Strut, strut, wobble.

Both poems from *The Thanksgiving Book* by Susan Higgins, Pumpkin Press, 1984. Used with permission.

Language Experience

Make Thanksgiving greeting cards, introducing new words such as harvest, gobble, wattles, Pilgrims, etc.

The children can color the cards and dictate their sentiments for inside the card. Bring some greeting cards and read them aloud. The children may want to model their card after some of these. You can also compose and design a giant card as a group to display.

Creative Dramatics

Go shopping for Thanksgiving dinner! Use empty food boxes, egg cartons, etc., and place them around the story space. One child wears an apron and is the store owner, who operates a pretend cash register. (Use a decorated box and a bell to "ring" up the items.) Play money and lists can also be used by the rest of the children, who are the "shoppers."

Have a turkey trot. Cut feather shapes out of construction paper and glue around the top of 9" paper plates like turkey feathers. Poke a hole in the plate and string yarn through. Tie the feathers on the waists of the children with the plate in back and the tie in front. Tell the children to pretend to be turkeys: squat down, flap their wings, and "gobble!" Have the children turkey trot around the area.

Literature-Based Activity: No Cook Turkeys

Supplies: One 8½" x 11" piece of light brown construction paper, crayons, scissors, popsicle stick, tape.
Directions: Each child traces their hand on the brown paper and cuts it out. Use the crayons to decorate the thumb as the turkey's head and the rest of the fingers as feathers. A small piece of red yarn could also be taped on for the wattles. Tape the turkey to the popsicle stick and use with the fingerplay.
Cost per turkey: 6¢

❏ Additional Literature Selections

Balian, Lorna. *Sometimes It's Turkey – Sometimes It's Feathers*. Abingdon, 1973.

Caitlin, Wynelle. *Old Wattles*. Doubleday, 1975.

Cohen, Miriam. *Don't Eat Too Much Turkey*. Dell, 1988.

Kroll, Stephen. *One Tough Turkey*. Holiday House, 1982.

Patent, Dorothy Hinshaw. *Wild Turkey, Tame Turkey*. Clarion, 1989.

Pilkey, Dav. *'Twas the Night Before Thanksgiving*. Orchard, 1990.

Reese, Bob. *Wild Turkey Run*. Aro Publishing, 1987.

Smith, Janice. *The Turkey's Side of It*. HarperCollins, 1992.

"The Turkey Girl," p. 45-52, from *Look Back and See* by Margaret Read MacDonald, HW Wilson, 1991.

Turkey Nametag

U is for Universe

Learn about the solar system, stars, and planets! Turn off the lights and use flashlights. Hang glittery stars from the ceiling.

Which Way to the Milky Way?
By Sidney Rosen. (Carolrhoda Books, 1992)

In a question and answer format, this book introduces kids to the Milky Way and other kinds of galaxies in the universe. Cartoon images are juxtaposed over observatory photographs for enjoyable illustrations. Includes a glossary.

❏ Warm-Up Activities

Fingerplay

Five Bright Stars

Five bright stars shining in the night
Shine in the universe with their light,
The first star shoots away,
The second star fades into day,
The third star hides behind the moon,
The fourth star shines into your room,
The fifth star shines, and you wonder why
So many stars shine in a night sky.

Music

Use *Journey Into Space* by Jane Murphy, Kimbo Educational Records, 1988.

"Adventures in Space" from *On the Move With Greg and Steve* by Greg Scelsa and Steve Millang, Micheal Brent Publications, 1987.

❏ Follow-Up Activities

Poetry

Stars

I looked up
and saw a star,
It looked so close
But was so far.

Sometimes
Stars fall,
But they can't be found
at all.

The stars
At night
Far away
So bright.

Language Experience

Send messages to outer space! Look up information on the gold disk sent into space on the Voyager 2 space probe. To get started, try looking up the Voyager in *The World Book Encyclopedia*. The disk is filled with sounds from the planet earth as well as a message of peace to extraterrestrials from former President Jimmy Carter. The children can make up their own packet of messages that they would send to space. Have them write or draw pictures.

Creative Dramatics

Children can pretend to be a shooting star, the sun, the moon, a nova, or their interpretation of any space body or phenomenon.

Or, have them pretend to be an extraterrestrial. How do they think it would walk or talk? What would it eat?

Use the book of creative drama about stars, *Skip Aboard a Space Ship* by Jane Moncure, Children's Press, 1978.

Literature-Based Activity: Star Gazers

Supplies: An empty round oatmeal box, scraps paper, glue, tracing paper, a pencil, scissors, markers, and a book of constellations for each gazer.
Directions: Take the lid off the oatmeal box and trace around the closed bottom of the box with the pencil onto the tracing paper. Look at the book of constellations and find one that you would like to make. Draw dots with the pencil inside the circle that represent the stars in your constellation. Turn the tracing paper

over so you can see the reverse of the constellation and place it over the closed end of the oatmeal box. Using the point of your pencil, poke holes through the oatmeal box where the dots are. Color the inside and outside bottom of the oatmeal box black using a black marker. Decorate the outside of the oatmeal box with scrap paper and markers. Hold the gazer up to a light source and view the stars!
Cost per gazer: 4¢

❑ Additional Literature Selections

Asimov, Isaac. *Mythology and the Universe.* Gareth Stevens, 1990.

Bendick, Jeanne. *The Universe: Think Big!* Milbrook Press, 1991.

George, Micheal. *Stars.* Creative Education, 1991.

Hall, Katy. *Spacey Riddles.* Dial, 1992.

Hist, Robin. *My Place in Space.* Orchard Books, 1990.

Leedy, Loreen. *Postcards from Pluto: A Tour of the Solar System.* Henry Holt, 1993.

Livingston, Myra Cohn. *Space Songs. Holiday House*, 1993.

Robinson, Fay. *Space Probes to the Planets.* Albert A. Whitman, 1993.

Rosen, Sidney. *How Far to a Star?* Carolrhoda Books, 1992.

Simon, Seymour. *Galaxies.* Morrow, 1988.

Yorinks, Arthur. *Company's Coming.* Crown, 1988.

Use "N" Nametag

V is for Volcano

A volcanic eruption is a spectacular but scary sight. There are volcanoes all over the world. Although they can be scary, volcanoes show scientists much about the earth's interior.

Surtsey: The Newest Place on Earth

By Katherine Lasky. (Hyperion Press, 1992)

The formation, naming, and colonization of a 27-year-old volcanic island named Surtsey. Explains how the first plants and animals were established. A beautiful photographic record of a fascinating event.

❏ Warm-Up Activities

Action Rhyme

A huge volcano,
Shaped like a "V"
(make and upside down "V" with your hands)
A mountain that is taller
Than a tall, tall tree.
(raise arms above head)
Mostly it is quiet,
(put finger to lips and say Shhhhh!)
But sometimes *Loud.*
(say the word loud very loudly)
And lava will always
Get rid of a crowd!

"The Little Mountain was Quiet and Asleep," from *Fingerplay Friends: Action Rhymes for Home, Church or School* by Audrey Leighton, Judson Press, 1984, p. 25.

Song

"Old Volcano"
(Sung to the tune of "Frere Jaques.")
Old volcano, old volcano,
Is asleep, is asleep.
(repeat)
Shh, now don't you wake him,
Shh, now don't you wake him.
He's asleep, he's asleep.
(clap loud to wake up volcano)

Old volcano, old volcano,
Is awake, is awake.
(stand up slowly)
(repeat)
Rumble, rumble, grumble,
Rumble, rumble, grumble,
He's blown his top,
He's blown his top!
(stretch out arms)

❏ Follow-Up Activities

Poetry

"V is for Volcano," from *Laughing Time* by W.J. Smith, Delacorte, 1980.

Language Experience

Pass out triangles cut from brown paper. Help the children to write a volcano shape poem following the outline of the triangle. This can be a descriptive or simply a sound poem.

Locate and label some famous volcanoes on a world map. Some volcanoes are Mount Vesuvius, Mount Etna, Mount Fuji, Kilimanjaro, Mount St. Helens, Mauna Loa, Mount Hood, and Paracutin.
Label a diagram of a volcano with the appropriate parts: crust, rim, magma, central vent, ash, and lava ash.

If a new volcano erupted in your town, what would you name it? Record the children's suggestions.

Creative Dramatics

Have the children act out the song "Old Volcano." Start out with the children still and quiet, and then they can make rumbling noises and movements as the volcano begins to erupt.

Literature-Based Activity: "Mount Librarius"

Supplies: To make "Mount Librarius," you will need clay or mud, one 6" paper plate, cotton balls, small stones, and red, orange, and yellow food coloring. If desired, use this mud recipe: One cup all purpose flour, ½ cup salt, ⅓ cup unsweetened cocoa powder, ½ cup water. Mix together flour, salt, and cocoa powder. Add water and stir until moistened. Lightly flour your hands and a flat surface. Knead until smooth.

Directions: Take your clay or mud and put a fistful on the paper plate. Use your hands to shape it into a volcano. Repeat with more mud until it is the desired size. To make lava, stretch a cotton ball over the sides of your volcano in a thin layer. Dribble food coloring over the top to color. Let "Mount Librarius" dry overnight.

Cost per volcano: 5¢

❏ Additional Literature Selections

Argueta, Malio. *The Magic Dogs of the Volcanoes.* Children's Book Press, 1990.

Carson, James. *Volcanoes.* Bookwright Press, 1984.

Challand, Helen. *Volcanoes.* Children's Press, 1988.

Dineen, Jaqueline. *Volcanoes.* Glouchester Press, 1991.

George, Micheal. *Volcanoes.* Creative Education, 1991.

Grifalconi, Ann. *The Village of Round and Square Houses.* Little Brown, 1986.

Kunhardt, Edith. *Pompeii...Buried Alive.* Random House, 1987.

Lewis, Thomas. *Hill of Fire.* Harper and Row, 1971.

Micheal, George. *Volcanoes.* Creative Education, 1991.

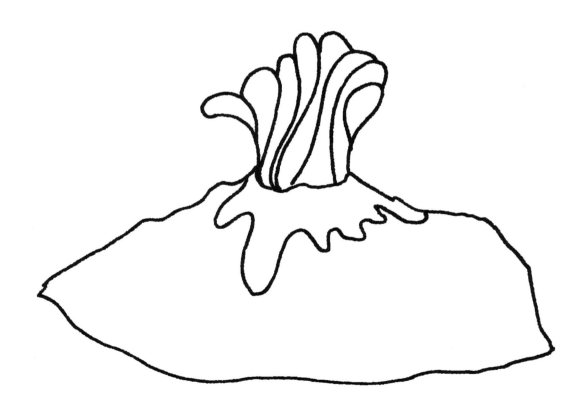

Volcano Nametag

 *is for* **Whale**

Children get a feel for life under the sea. Use a large cardboard box or borrow a real boat and fill it with pillows. Tell the children to "Get in to the swim" of reading.

Winter Whale

By Joanne Ryder. (Morrow, 1991)

An imaginative tale told from the point of view of a boy who pretends he is a whale. Poetic descriptions of whale life are accompanied by beautiful illustrations. Of special note are the whale-shaped clouds found throughout the book.

❏ Warm-Up Activities

5 Whales

Five whales swimming in the sea.
The blue whale said, "The sea is for me!"
The humpback said, "The sea is deep."
The beluga said, "It's where we sleep."
The narwhale said, "We swim and dip."
The sperm whale said, "We swim with ships."
Then all the whales spouts went "Swoosh!"
And they jumped in the air with a splash and a sploosh.

Songs

"The Whales are Talking" from *Grandpa Art Sings About Sea Creatures* by Arthur Custer, Sun Group, 1993.

Whales, Whales, Whales by Fred Gee, Clear Horizons Music, 1991.

"A Whale Vacation," from *What's in the Sea* by Lois Skiera-Zucek, Kimbo Educational, 1990.

❏ Follow-Up Activities

Poetry

Would you like
To be a whale
Swimming in the sea?
A large whale
From mouth to tail

With a spout
That looks like rain.
Would you love to swallow
Great oceans of water
And wallow about
With the sea as your home?

Language Experience

Such a gigantic creature invites a child's imagination to run wild. Give the children some story starters and let them tell, write or illustrate their whale tale. An example of a starter is "One day while fishing, I felt a strange tug on my line..."

Creative Dramatics

The children can create a whale with their bodies. In a large area, assign each student a part of the whale's body. Some can be ribs, fins and the tail. Others can be the mouth and the spout. Have all the children practice making the whooshing sound of the spout. On your signal, have the children stand together and make their parts move.

Use the book of creative drama *A Beach in My Bedroom* by Jane Moncure, Children's Press, 1978.

Literature-Based Activities: Cup Whale

Supplies: One paper cup, pattern, a 2 ½ x 3½ piece of blue construction paper, scissors, tape, and a straw.
Directions: Cut out the copy of the whale pattern and color as desired. Tape the whale to the front of the cup. Cut a fringe in the blue construction paper. Roll it around one end of the straw and attach with tape. Punch a hole in the bottom of the cup with a pencil and insert a straw. Move the straw up and down to make spout work. For more fun, blow bubbles as you manipulate the whale puppet.
Cost per whale: 5¢

At the Beach

Use any of the seashore books listed below. Have the children bring beach towels, swimsuits, a sack lunch, and sunglasses from home. Borrow a small wading pool, sea shells, a beach umbrella, and even some sand. Have children spread out their towels and have a beach party while listening to stories.

Soap Waves

Draw a whale on blue construction paper. Mix some powdered soap flakes with a little water to form a paste. Finger paint the paste on the paper to form waves around the whale.
Cost: Free

❏ Additional Literature Selections

Allen, Judy. *Whale.* Candlewick Press, 1992.

Crema, Laura. *Look Inside the Ocean.* Grosset and Dunlap, 1992.

James, Simon. *Dear Mr. Blueberry.* Margaret K. McElderry, 1991.

Johnston, Tony. *Whale Song.* Putnam, 1987.

"Juanita the Whale," p. 38-43, from *Draw and Tell by Richard Thompson*, Annick Press, 1988.

McFarlane, Sheryl. *Waiting for the Whales.* Philomel, 1993.

Paraskevas, Betty. *On the Edge of the Sea.* Dial, 1992.

Patent, Dorothy Hinshaw. *Killer Whales.* Holiday House, 1993.

"Wally and Wilma," p. 70-75, from *Cut and Tell Scissor Stories for Spring* by Jean Warren, Totline Press, 1984.

Weller, Frances. *I Wonder If I'll See a Whale.* Philomel, 1991.

Zotolow, Charlotte. *The Seashore Book.* Harper Collins, 1992.

Whale Nametag

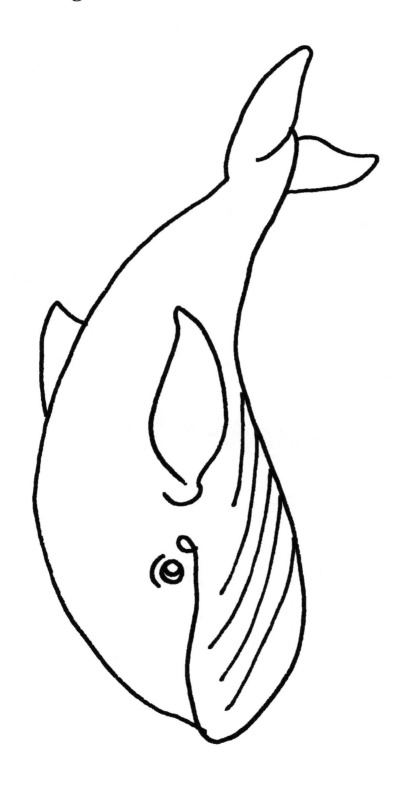

Cup Whale

 *is for* **Xeric**

Xeric is a word that means adapted to an extremely dry habitat. Here are some desert plants and animals.

A Walk in the Desert

By Caroline Arnold. (Silver Press, 1990)

This book describes the plants, animals, and conditions of the dry, hot desert. Cactus types, birds, lizards, rabbits, owls, and bats are included. A map of deserts of the world is included.

❑ Warm-Up Activities

Fingerplay

Five tarantulas walking by,
Four vultures up in the sky.
Three lizards on a rock,
Two roadrunners give a squawk.
One baby scorpion scuttles away,
That is what I saw in the desert today!
(Hold up 5,4,3,2,1 fingers)

Song

"Desert Creatures" by Tamara Hunt from *A Pocketful of Puppets* by Tamara Hunt, Nancy Renfro Studios, 1984, p. 42. (PO Box 164226, Austin, TX 78716.) Used with permission.

Desert Creatures

Tarantulas walk
Jack rabbits hop
But when sidewinders slither
I stop!
Wolves bay
Owls hoot
But when coyotes howl
I scoot!
Centipedes crawl
Scorpions scurry
But when gila monsters tarry
I hurry!
Road runners run
Vultures glide
But when hawks hover

I hide!
Lizards leap
Beetles squeak
But when rattlesnakes shake
I SHRIEK!

❑ Follow-Up Activities

Poetry

The book *Desert Voices* by Byrd Baylor and Peter Parnall (Scribner's, 1981) is filled with lovely poetry about the creatures who live in the desert.
Also use the poem "This is No Place," by Byrd Baylor from *Go With the Poem*, Lillian Moore, McGraw Hill, 1979.

Language Experience

Do a choral reading of the following poem.

The Desert

Chorus: It's hot, it's dry!
Girls: I don't know why....
Boys: Take off your hat! It's too dry to cry!
Solo: Whew! It's hot!
Girls: Let's not...
Solo: Whew! It's hot!
Girls: ...stay, let's go!
Boys: And find some snow!
Chorus: It's hot! It's dry! Goodbye!

Creative Dramatics

As you do the above choral reading, assign some children to dramatize as the chorus reads. It might also be fun to use real hats, fans and an empty canteen.

Literature-Based Activity: Desert Creature Puppet

Supplies: One 9" paper plate, yarn, markers, one large paper sack, scissors, and tape.
Directions: Have the children help each other to put the paper plates on their faces and make small marks

for eye holes. Take the plate and cut out holes to see through. Have the children choose a desert creatures from the book *A Walk in the Desert* or from the poem "Desert Creatures." Decorate the mask to be the animal they choose. The sack can also be decorated and cut out for the body. Attach to the mask with tape. Poke a hole on each side of the mask and tie yarn in the holes. Tie the yarn around the child's head to wear the mask. Animals to suggest are buzzard, badger, coyote, fox, snake, toad, rabbit.
Cost per puppet: 10¢

❏ Additional Literature Selections

Bash, Barbara. *Desert Giant*. Sierra Club, 1989.

Baylor, Byrd. *The Desert Voices*. Scribners, 1981.

Guiberson, Brenda. *Cactus Hotel*. Henry holt, 1991.

John, Naomi. *Roadrunner*. Dutton, 1980.

Lerner, Carol. *A Desert Year*. Morrow, 1991.

Mora, Pat. *Listen to the Desert/Oye al Desierto.* Clarion, 1994.

Pearce, Q. L. N*ature's Footprints in the Desert.* Silver Press, 1990.

Siebert, Diane. *Mojave.* Crowell, 1988.

Use"R" Nametag

 *is for Yolk*

Save eggshells from cooking, wash and dry, and draw faces with markers. Fill with soil and some grass seed. Sprinkle with water. Place shells on upside down bottle caps by a window. They will sprout "hair" in a few days.

Eggs on Your Nose
By Ann McGovern. (Macmillan, 1987)

A story in rhyming verse of the utter and complete mess a child makes while eating eggs alone for the first time.

❑ Warm-Up Activities

Fingerplays

Five Eggs

Five eggs and five eggs,
(hold up two hands)
That makes ten.
Sitting on top is the mother hen.
(fold one hand over the other)
Crackle, crackle, crackle;
(clap three times)
What do I see?
Ten fluffy chickens
(hold up ten fingers)
As yellow as can be!

Counting Eggs

How many eggs can your basket hold?
(pretend to hold basket on arm)
One, two, three, four
(pretend to put eggs in basket)
Now put in some more
Five, six, seven, eight
That's a lot, you're doing great!
Get some more, try again.
Two more, and that makes ten.
(hold up ten fingers)

❑ Follow-Up Activities

Poetry

"Egg Thoughts" by Russell Hoban from *Egg Thoughts and Other Frances Songs*, Harper and Row, 1972, p. 6.

Egg Thoughts
Soft Boiled

I do not like the way you slide,
I do not like your soft inside,
I do not like you many ways,
And I could go for many days
Without a soft boiled egg.

Sunny Side Up

With their yolks and whites all runny
They are looking at me funny.

Sunny Side Down

Lying face down on the plate
On their stomachs there they wait.

Poached

Poached eggs on toast, why do you shiver
With such a funny little quiver?

Scrambled

I eat as well as I am able,
But some falls underneath the table.

Hard Boiled

With so much suffering today
Why do them any other way?

Riddle

In marble walls
As white as milk

Lined with a skin
As soft as silk.
Within a fountain
Crystal clear
A golden apple
Does appear.
No doors are there
To this stronghold
Yet thieves break in
And steal the gold.
(An Egg!)

Creative Dramatics

Do a rotten egg fight in pantomime! It's morning on the farm, and the eggs are ready to be harvested. Suddenly, an egg hits you on the arm! Play the pantomime egg game twice, once with each side winning.

Have children pretend to be inside an egg. First, they roll up in a ball, then "Peck, peck, peck," on the shell. Next, break out all wet and bedraggled. Shake dry, fluff their feathers, take tiny chick steps and say "Peep, peep."

Language Experience

Make up some fun word that begin with the letters E-G-G. Some ideas are *egg*citing, *egg*stra, *egg*sample. Print them on tagboard for everyone to see.

Cut some 5" tall egg shapes from white paper. Cut some picture of animals that hatch from eggs out of old magazines. Cut the egg shapes in half across the middle and give the cut edge a "cracked" look. Attach the two paper egg pieces together on one side using a paper fastener. Tape the creatures to the back of the bottom half of the eggs so their heads appear when you "crack" the eggs by swinging the top piece up. The names of the animals can be written on the egg as the children identify them.

Literature-Based Activity: No Yolk Baby Chicks

Supplies: Pattern, two cotton balls, yellow construction paper, a black marker or crayon, glue, scissors.
Directions: Trace the pattern for the beak, feet, eyes, and wings on the yellow construction paper and cut out. Glue the two cotton balls together, one is the head and one is the body. Let the glue dry. Glue the beak, feet, wings, and eyes to the cotton balls and let dry. An egg cup cut from an egg carton can be used as an egg for the chick.
Cost per chick: 6¢

❏ Additional Literature Selections

Auch, Mary Jane. *The Easter Egg Farm.* Holiday House, 1992.

Baker, Keith. *Big Fat Hen.* Harcourt Brace Jovanovich, 1994.

Barber, Antonia. *Gemma and the Baby Chick.* Scholastic, 1993.

De Burgoing, Pascale. *The Egg.* Scholastic, 1992.

"E," p. 21-23, from *Paper-Cutting Stories from A to Z* by Valerie Marsh, Alleyside Press, 1992.

Heller, Ruth. *Chickens Aren't the Only Ones.* Grossett and Dunlap, 1981.

Joyce, William. *Bently and Egg.* HarperCollins, 1992.

Lionni, Leo. *An Extraordinary Egg.* Knopf, 1994.

"A Penny and A Half," p. 157-160, from *Look Back and See* by Margaret Read MacDonald, HW Wilson, 1991.

Ross, Tom. Eggbert, *The Slightly Cracked Egg.* G.P. Putnam, 1994.

"William and Warble," p. 80-85, from *Draw and Tell* by Richard Thompson, Annick Press, 1988.

Ziefert, Harriet. *Egg Drop Day.* Little Brown, 1988.

No Yolk Baby Chick

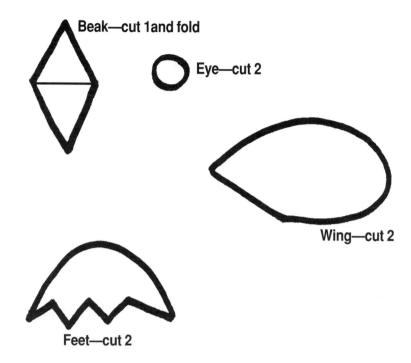

Beak—cut 1and fold

Eye—cut 2

Wing—cut 2

Feet—cut 2

Yolk Nametag

Z *is for* **Zebra**

Have a zebra day. Wear all black and white. Use only black and white paper and crayons. Serve vanilla ice cream with oreos—Zebra Sundaes!

Greedy Zebra

By Mwyene Hadithi. (Little Brown, 1984)

An explanation in folklore of why zebras have stripes. Long ago, all the animals were a dull and dusty color. Then the heavens bring forth furs, skins, and horns of many colors. All the animals are eager to try on their new clothes, except for zebra, who is too busy eating. All that is left is a small swatch of black cloth that does not quite fit.

❏ **Warm-Up Activities**

Song

I Am a Zebra
(To the tune of "I'm A Little Teapot")
I am a zebra, white and black,
I have so many stripes upon my back
In Africa, on the plains, I play all day
And if a lion comes, I'll run away.

   "A Zebra is Just a Donkey With Stripes," from *Zippity Zoo Day* by Derrie Frost, Melody House, 1989.

Fingerplay

Five Zebras

Five zebras in the zoo door.
One ran away and then there were four.
Four zebras saying "Neeee, neee!"
One jumped away and then there were three.
Three zebras, here's someone new,
It's a lion! Now there are two.
Two zebras, watch them run.
One was faster, now there is one.
One zebra, looking for his friends.
The zebras all came back again!

❏ **Follow-Up Activities**

Poetry

The Donkey and the Zebra (Traditional)

When the donkey
Saw the zebra
He began
To switch his tail.
"Well, I never,"
Said the donkey,
"There's a mule
That's been to jail!"

Language Experience

Have the children illustrate an animal alphabet. Each child may be assigned a letter to draw, or they can choose their animal. Assemble the pictures into book form and label with appropriate letter, or laminate and make a set of animal flashcards.

Creative Dramatics

On page 59 of *Let's Find the Big Idea* is a playlet called "The Law of the Jungle" that has a zebra and several other African animals as characters. This could be done as a choral reading, a play for the children to watch, or one they act themselves.
Use the book *Walking Through the Jungle* and make stick puppets for the children to hold as you share the story. Each child can make the animal noise of the puppet they hold. The same can be done with *Polar Bear, Polar Bear, What Do You Hear?*

Literature-Based Activity: Greedy Zebras

Supplies: Copy pattern for each child. Give them crayons.
Directions: Tell the children to illustrate what Zebra might have looked like had he not spent so much time eating, Would he have horns or fur? What color would he be? They can be imaginative. The activity can be expanded by bringing in samples of different fabrics for the children to touch and look at.
Cost per zebra: 1¢

❏ Additional Literature Selections

Arnold, Caroline. *Zebra*. Morrow, 1987.

Green, Carl. *Zebra*. Crestwood House, 1988.

Hefter, Richard. *Zip Goes Zebra*. Holt, 1981.

Hendrick, Mary Jane. *If Anything Ever Goes Wrong at the Zoo*. Harcourt, 1993.

Irvine, Georgeanne. *Zelda the Zebra*. Children's Press, 1982.

Lacome, Julie. *Walking Through the Jungle*. Candlewick, 1993.

Martin, Bill. *Polar Bear, Polar Bear, What Do You Hear?* Holt, 1991.

Medearis, Angela. *Zebra Riding Cowboy*. Henry Holt, 1992.

Peet, Bill. *Zella, Zack, and Zodiac*. Houghton Mifflin, 1986.

Stone, Lynn. *Zebras*. Rourke, 1990.

Van Curen, Barbara. *When Zebras Came for Lunch*. Lucky Books, 1989 (PO Box 1415, Winchester, VA 22604).

Vargo, Vanessa. *Zebra Talk*. Child's Play, 1991 (310 W. 47th Street, Apt 3D, New York, NY 10036-3153. 1-800-472-0099).

Zebra Nametag

Greedy Zebra

Bibliography

Useful resources for your literature-based activity library. Although some of these titles are out of print, they are available in public library professional or children's collections.

Books

Bay, Jeanette Graham. *A Treasury of Flannelboard Stories.* Alleyside Press, 1994.

Briggs, Diane. *Flannel Board Fun: A Collection of Stories, Songs, and Poems.* Scarecrow, 1992.

Carlson, Bernice Wells. *Let's Find the Big Idea.* Abingdon, 1982.

Colville, Josephine. *The Zoo Comes to School: Fingerplays and Action Rhymes.* Macmillan, 1973.

Dowell, Ruth. *Move Over Mother Goose.* Gryphon House, 1987.

Faber, Norma. *These Small Stones.* Harper and Row, 1987.

Gardner, John *A Child's Bestiary.* Alfred A. Knopf, 1977.

Knight, Joan. *Tickle Toe Rhymes.* Orchard, 1989.

Lewis, Patrick J. *Two Legged, Four Legged, No Legged Rhymes.* Knopf, 1991.

Lillegard, Dee. *September to September: Poems All Year.* Children's Press, 1986.

McCord, David. *One At a Time.* Little Brown, 1986.

Prelutsky, Jack, ed. *The Random House Book of Poetry for Children.* Random House, 1983.

———. *Read Aloud Rhymes for the Very Young.* Knopf, 1986.

———. *Zoo Doings.* Greenwillow, 1983.

Rosetti, Christina. *A Child's First Book of Poems.* Western Publishing. 1981.

Cassettes

Beall, Pamela. *Wee Sing Children's Songs and Fingerplays.* Price Stern Sloan, 1979.

Custer, Arthur. *Grandpa Art Sings About Sea Creatures.* Sun Group, 1993.

———. *Grandpa Art Sings Insect Songs.* Sun Group, 1993.

Livingston, Bob. *Open the Window.* Gentle Wind, 1991.

Murphy, Jane. *Journey into Space.* Kimbo Educational. 1988.

Palmer, Hap. *Animal Antics.* Activity Records, 1986.

Polansky, David. *Animal Alphabet Songs.* Perfect Score Music, 1982.

Sharon, Lois, and Bram. *Mainly Mother Goose.* Elephant Records, 1984.